R&D Your School:
How to Start, Grow, and Sustain
Your School's Innovation Engine

R&D Your School:
How to Start, Grow, and Sustain Your School's Innovation Engine

"Here's the question: What is potentially one of the greatest sources of energy on the planet?
Answer: Human Ingenuity.
Follow-up Question: What consumes more energy than almost anything else?
Answer: Our ongoing battle to maintain the status quo."

- Gary Marx, *21 Trends for the 21st Century*

American School of Bombay
SF 2, G Block, Bandra Kurla Complex Road,
Bandra East, Mumbai - 400 098.
INDIA

Email: publications@asbindia.org
www.asbindia.org

ISBN
Print Version: 978-1-4951-6152-0

Design by American School of Bombay

The Service mark Re.D Studio is the property of American School of Bombay

CONTENTS

FOREWORD

In late 2011, I had just finished writing a book about innovation in education. My research and classroom observations convinced me that a key to unlocking innovation in students is making sure that educators have opportunities to be innovators themselves. For this to happen, school systems need to be more tolerant of risk-taking, better connected to the world outside the classroom, and able to look ahead to anticipate the future benefits—and consider the drawbacks—of emerging ideas. In short, schools need to get more strategic about innovation.

By coincidence, I spent several weeks that fall in India, working with schools that were interested in project-based learning. One of my last stops was the American School of Bombay (ASB), an international school in Mumbai. I met with a team of teachers who had been researching PBL and were starting to implement projects with their students. I remember being impressed by their intellectual curiosity and their willingness to consider different ways of engaging today's learners. I noticed that they used the language of innovation to talk about prototyping, iterating, and scaling. It was also clear that these teachers had the full support of the leadership team. Indeed, school leaders were counting on them for recommendations to guide future PBL efforts.

As you'll see in the coming chapters, ASB doesn't just talk about the importance of innovation; it advances new ideas by bolting research and development—R&D—right into the institutional framework.

ASB established a Research and Development Department in 2011 to formalize its approach to innovation. R&D efforts have focused on a variety of hot topics in education, from PBL and the maker movement to reimagining the physical spaces for learning and rethinking the school calendar. Across diverse topics, ASB uses core innovation processes—explore, study, prototype, research, scale—to guide the work and set the stage for action. By inviting participation from across the school community, including teachers, parents, and students, ASB ensures that diverse perspectives inform future decisions.

In many ways, the R&D efforts underway here echo the processes that drive innovation in the world outside education. That's not to say that innovation doesn't happen in the education sector. It's just that we often find it happening under the radar, in isolated pockets or in individual classrooms. Meanwhile, traditional school systems tend to remain traditional—and slow or even resistant to change. In contrast, ASB has created a system to accelerate change from within. By sharing its insights with this book, ASB is opening its innovation toolkit for others to borrow and adapt. That's how good ideas will spread across the education sector.

Here's just a sampling: a Global Social Entrepreneurship Summit led by students for students, an immersive inquiry experience called Studio 6, and the use of learning analytics to personalize learning. Amid these fresh ideas, however, ASB manages to maintain the day-to-day consistency that students, parents, and educators expect from a learning environment. Change happens, to be sure, but not just for the sake of change. You'll hear in the coming pages about the "dual operating system" that allows for both consistency and disruption in education.

One of the hallmarks of an innovative idea is that it creates a new normal. Think about the breakthrough products that you can't imagine living without and the new ways of working that are already transforming society—from mobile devices to crowd sourcing platforms to ride-sharing services to whatever tomorrow brings.

With its thoughtful yet bold approach to R&D, American School of Bombay has created a new normal for innovation in education. This publication continues the cycle by sharing what works, acknowledging challenges, and inviting others to take up the story and write their own new chapters.

Suzie Boss
Portland, Oregon, USA
May 2015

INTRODUCTION

This is not a book of good ideas. This is a book about how to take what is often an abstraction, sporadic activity, or talk - School Innovation – and show how research and development has been done at our school, the American School of Bombay, and how it could be done at your school. But before we go any further, we think it is important that we define what we mean when we say "innovation". Based on work by Rogers, we define 'innovation' as bringing an idea, practice, or object perceived as new to an individual, a team, an organization, or community in order to meet important learning needs (Rogers, 2003).

Established in 1981, the American School of Bombay (ASB) is a Pre-K to Grade 12 school located in Mumbai, India. While ASB is a U.S. style school, the Indian setting and its multi-national community, representing over 50 countries, brings together children who have varied experiences to learn in a dynamic and engaging environment. As an International Baccalaureate World School, the school's PYP, Middle School, Pre-IB, and IB Diploma programs perfectly complement our American curriculum and prepare students for other international schools as well as college and university. Innovation and a forward-looking perspective have been a part of the school's DNA since 2002, when it became one of the first PreK-12 laptop/tablet programs among overseas American schools. Today, grounded in its mission to inspire and empower students, ASB aggressively works to make its vision for the future a reality. This vision is to provide the most relevant educational experience in a highly collaborative and individualized context. Change at ASB is powered by its dual operating system of Teaching & Learning and Research & Development. Our Teaching & Learning operating system ensures that we deliver the most relevant and research-proven instruction to our students, across all grade levels, every day. Our Research & Development operating system shifts the horizon of what is possible in schools through trend analysis, prototyping, and conducting original research. ASB's dual operating system creates a culture of inquiry that fosters curiosity and encourages risk-taking by providing opportunities for students, parents, faculty and staff to challenge themselves in classroom and real-world contexts.

In 2011, the ASB created a Research and Development (R&D) operating system to explore, study, prototype, research, and scale new practices, approaches, and systems for the future of our students. That decision, and the work that many hands have carried forward since, have become part of our everyday in 2015. Our failures, the insights we've gleaned from them, and the learning we've taken from our successes over the past four years, have created successful results that are impacting our students. This learning, the committed collaboration and leadership of our colleagues in R&D work, and the results that have impacted our students at ASB have made us ardent believers in school-based, school-led innovation.

In considering the future in their book, *The Reciprocity Advantage*, Bob Johansen and Karl Ronn describe the change environment of the next decade as a 'VUCA world on Steroids' where:

"**Volatility** will call out for **Vision**
Uncertainty will call out for **Understanding**
Complexity will call out for **Clarity**
Ambiguity will call out for **Agility**"

(Johansen & Ronn, 2014, pp. 64-65)

We believe that a Research and Development department enables schools to sustain relevance in a VUCA world. We wouldn't be able to write this book in good faith if we hadn't experienced our R&D department enabling ASB to:

Create compelling **visions** for our future
Expand our **understanding** of our learner's needs
Gather insights that result in **clarity** for determining directions and making decisions
Develop capacity to take action with **agility** to meet our learners' needs.

At the end of our fourth year of R&D at ASB, work that was once undertaken for the future's sake has become incorporated in the present. What was once a report on 21st century school design has become school buildings, classrooms, and furniture designed to foster learning engagement for our students. What began as study and research of alternative school-year calendars, has resulted in a revamped school calendar with 265 days of school, an ASB Intersessions program, and a vision and action plans for the future of professional learning. We are transforming one prototype at a time. The speed, agility, and focus of a school R&D operating system have enabled us to harness the change environment to create new innovations that result in relevant learning for our students. We're still learning, increasingly aware that there are important opportunities and transformations whose surface we haven't scratched yet. But we also believe that relevant learning for students in a rapid-change VUCA world begins at schools with the capacity for fast, agile, focused innovation.

Why did we write this book?
We are often asked for guidance on how to create a sustainable system for school innovation. This book is an attempt to answer those questions. We think you should read this book primarily with *your* school in mind and a pen & paper or a laptop so that you can start to capture your thoughts, ideas, and inner dialog about how what you are reading can lead to school innovation in your context. We have focused on using real-school illustrations of R&D work to show how systematic research and development has occurred at the American School of Bombay. Our hope is that reading about *our* system for school research and development, equips and inspires you to adopt, adapt, hack, or to otherwise create *your* own system for school research and development to sustain innovation for relevant learning for your students.

Why R&D Your School?
The need for innovation is moving to the front of the line at our schools. Our shared future is coming at us with increasing speed, but the structures that have been our strength are not built for the agility, speed, and focus that schools need to meet the pace of change. Schools and school leaders around the world are looking to innovation to create and develop the schools that students need. This year's National Association of Independent Schools (NAIS) Conference focused on Innovation and Design exhorting school leaders to "Design the Revolution". In March, over 50 international schools gathered at the Graded School in Sao Paulo, Brazil, for the Innovate 2015 conference to focus and learn how to engage in "Re-imagining School."

Innovation is no longer for futurists or the avant garde predicting an abstract future or pushing the envelope for what may eventually be possible in schools. It's something we can see the need for in our daily lives. As the gap between the way students live and the way they learn at school widens, we are increasingly confronted by more needs, questions, and opportunities than we are structured to engage with.

We chose to call it "Research and Development" instead of "Innovation". That has been an important choice. We viewed R&D as standing for concrete, deliberate, evidence-based, collaborative future making for a domain. On the other hand, Innovation seemed to be perceived as being ethereal, incidental, and the domain of lone geniuses.

What's In this Book?

R&D Your School is written for schools and school leaders that are looking for that system -- a system for sustained innovation to meet the needs of their students for relevant learning in a rapidly accelerating change environment. At its core, this book provides a simple structure, eight essential conditions for successful R&D in schools, and a set of strategic actions that can drive fast, agile, focused, and systematic research and development of new high-impact opportunities at any school. In this book you will find out about:

- The impacts of R&D at ASB
- The dual operating system structure that enables school R&D
- The essential conditions for successful R&D in schools
- Prototyping in schools
- Accelerators for school R&D work
- Case studies that illustrate R&D work in schools
- Resources for R&D work in schools

As you read about our work, our missteps, and the adjustments we've made to grow innovation capacity at ASB, we hope you will find useful structures, ideas, insights and tools that enable you to begin growing, developing and improving on our work to build the R&D system that your school and students require for their future.

Finally, the pages of this book are chock-full of the contributions of volunteers of educators participating in R&D work. Several chapters have been written by these faculty volunteers. The energy, passion, and thinking they have contributed in pursuit of innovation at ASB over the past four years has been truly astonishing. This book is dedicated, with gratitude, to the crowd of volunteer innovators who R&D our school.

Shabbi Luthra
Director of Research &
Development

Scot Hoffman
Research & Development
Coordinator

CHAPTER 1

EDUCATIONAL MALPRACTICE

(This chapter is written by Craig Johnson, Superintendent of ASB)

"If a teacher is ONLY using the same resources and teaching the same skills they were using five years ago, they are guilty of educational malpractice." Suan Yeo, Google Education Evangelist.

Michel Zappa, a technology-futurist, recently said, "Today is the slowest day you will have for the rest of your life." He went on to illustrate how every day will be slower than the days that follow it. The "collective global knowledge (CGK)," and our ability to access this information, is growing at an exponential rate. I read somewhere, recently, that there are approximately 750 million pictures of cats on the internet. I'm a dog lover and a consumer of this CGK. As such, I will never need a picture of a cat. The fact that there are 750 million pictures of cats means nothing to me since I will make no attempt to access it. The pictures of cats don't bother me and I will leave them alone. We can happily coexist, neither of us adding value nor stress to the other's life. But, for those cat lovers this is a valuable amount of information to have access to. I wish them the best.

"At the end of 2012," Zappa added, "It was calculated that 'three days worth of new content' was made accessible on the web every sixty seconds." In other words: Every minute we are bombarded with (or at least have access to) three days' worth of information that we didn't have a minute earlier which (according to my math: 3x60x24=4320 days OR 11.84 years) means almost 12 years worth of 'new content is accessible' to us every day. Mr. Zappa's conclusions thrilled and scared me.

Why was I scared? Because I'm an educator. My job, as it has always existed, is deeply rooted in knowledge, content, skills, and access. This is scary. Why was I thrilled? Because I'm an educator. My job is to create structures that allow children to learn. This is thrilling.

Jose Ferreira, Founder and CEO of *Knewton* (an adaptive learning platform) writes: "When you look back at history, all the great moments that defined the human race were about education: Greco-Roman civilization, the Renaissance, and the Industrial Revolution. I'm convinced that we're on the verge of the fourth big revolution." I agree. Revolutions, in the simplest of terms, take place when the status quo becomes irrelevant. Schools as they exist today are, for the most part, irrelevant. Mr. Suan Yeo, a Google Education Evangelist lists the following "things about schools" that students will not need when they graduate in 2020:

- *How to Use a Mo use:* Most high school seniors will no longer recognize the term: computer mouse.
- *Memorizing MLA and APA Style Requirements:* Open source programs and sites provide easier and better ways for 'correct style' to be achieved.
- *How to Find Reference Materials in the Library:* Skills necessary to make the "libraries of the 21st century" useful are very different than picking up a reference book and thumbing through it.
- *Developing Film, Taking the Perfect Picture:* Education is no longer about how to take the perfect picture. It's about responsible use of images and how to judge which of the thousands of pictures (remember my earlier data point about the cats?) we take are good ones.
- *How to Read a Paper Map:* The density of GPS units and the accessibility to them has made this skill obsolete.
- *Memorizing formulas:* Even the most basic technology will eliminate the need for any formulas or equations to be memorized.

Mr. Yeo adds, "If a teacher is ONLY using the same resources and teaching the same skills they were using five years ago, they are guilty of educational malpractice."

I think the keyword in Yeo's quote (and the word that saved his credibility with an audience of teachers) is "ONLY". We all know that there are some resources and skills that are eternal. Finding out which ones should stay and which ones should go, as an educator and a parent, is the tough part (albeit important and fun). Schools that find the right answer will remain relevant—a mantra that is becoming a rather ubiquitous echo in ASB's collective head.

In his book *Linchpin*, Seth Godin declares that "average is over." Godin contends that being "remarkable" means being generous, creating art, making judgment calls, and connecting people and ideas. ASB would agree. One of the most powerful driving forces behind ASB, as an educational institution, is our community's passionate commitment to BEING RELEVANT. The world we live in is morphing and mashing-up. We live in an interdisciplinary world where the advantage ALWAYS goes to the agile Do-It-Yourself (DIY) learners who know how to learn effectively and team with others. School MUST recognize and appreciate this reality, and respond accordingly. Researching and developing new instructional prototypes that model inquiry, thought, dreaming, and action will allow us to remain relevant for the learners we serve.

So, what are some of the things pushing us toward irrelevancy? Terry Heick, Director of Curriculum at *TeachThought* says these are five things *Education Does Today That Will Embarrass Us In 25 Years*:
- Vacations: Why do we feel the need to provide months off at a time from learning and structured thinking.
- Being blinded by data, research, and strategies: Why can't we see that communities, emotions, and habits really drive learning.
- Reporting progress with report cards: If we try other ways parents get confused and downright feisty. Schools do a poor job helping parents understand what grades really mean, and so they insist on the formats they grew up with.
- Holding parent conferences only twice a year: What? And still not all parents show up. Schools SHOULD completely freak out if 100% of parents don't attend.

- Ignoring apprenticeships: An apprenticeship is a powerful form of personalized learning that completely marries "content," performance, craft, and communities.

I recently sent the following question to one hundred and fifty Heads of Schools around the world: *What is the most important and relevant challenge facing international schools?* There was an overwhelming consensus, among respondents, that the #1 challenge is: *A Shortage of Highly Effective 21st Century Teachers.*

What exactly does that mean? Well, here's my analysis of the data: Once upon a time, schools were places where students went to be taught 'content' from 'content-experts.' In this context, content means: the what, where, when and who of things. And once upon a time, that was a good thing. However, today's landscape, of what students need to learn (not to mention 'how' they learn), has completely transformed. This transformation has resulted in a shortage of properly trained and appropriately equipped teachers. Literally, there is a 'supply' shortage of teachers that can effectively deliver on the 'demand' of what schools need to provide and what students need to learn.

According to one respondent, "The battle 'schools for the future' are fighting is finding the 'right' balance between content and skills." I think we would all agree, that neither content nor skills are worth very much without the other. And, there is no doubt, that the incorrect emphasis of one over the other will leave students disadvantaged. Another Head of School said, "When hiring teachers today we need to ensure that they have a mastery of their content, but also that they are highly capable of modeling, teaching, and assessing the right skills." He went on to say, "For every ten teachers [in my current school or from the pool of candidates I have interviewed in the past few years] only two, in my opinion, could effectively design the right educational environment to facilitate deep skill-learning for their students." In other words, there's an 80% mismatch between supply and demand. Filling that gap is, in the opinion of more than a hundred International School Heads, the most important challenge facing our schools as we head towards 2020.

And so, if you've read this entire piece (with an open mind and a spirit curious for a truth) you too should be scared and thrilled. The challenge is colossal, the opportunities countless, and the work most critical. I believe Jose Ferreira is correct. We are at the dawn of a revolution. But, make no mistake: Our revolution is not against Education; it is for it. Education is and always will be our comrade. She stands with us, shoulder to shoulder, ready to fight. Yes, she is disheartened and sad...as are we. The revolution is late in coming and slow in building up its momentum. As the future crashes upon us, Education looks fondly upon her past but knows, only too well, it is time for her to evolve. The box we call "schools" in which we have shoved the concept of "education" is irrelevant. Education wants out. She is ready and willing. What approaches is a battle for the strong, the passionate, and the committed; not for the meek or weak, or for those that sleep. Education knows this and so do we. To all educational-revolutionaries and to Education herself (that immortal and treasured corner-stone of mankind) I offer this: An encouraging and inspirational excerpt from Rudyard Kipling's poem "If."

If you can keep your head when all about you
Are losing theirs and blaming it on you;
If you can trust yourself when all men doubt you,
But make allowance for their doubting too;
If you can dream---and not make dreams your master;
If you can bear to hear the truth you've spoken
Twisted by knaves to make a trap for fools,
Or watch the things you gave your life to, broken,
And stoop and build'em up with worn-out tools;
If you can force your heart and nerve and sinew
To serve your turn long after they are gone,
And so hold on when there is nothing in you
Except the Will which says to them: "Hold on!"
If you can fill the unforgiving minute
With sixty seconds' worth of distance run,
Yours is the Earth and everything that's in it,
And---which is more---you'll be a Man, my son!

CHAPTER 2

R&D Your School

It is a typical day in the Re.D Studio, home base for the Research and Development department at the American School of Bombay. The long table in the center of the office holds cups of stationery supplies, tilting stacks of books, computer cords, journal articles, building materials, screwdrivers, a staple gun, and laptops. This is where the R&D department explores, researches and develops new teaching practices, approaches, and systems for schools.

This morning two elementary students have cornered the game developers/makers on our team and engaged them in a conversation about modding their Minecraft worlds and programming, before their attention shifts to the nearly completed drone kit that sits near the entrance of the studio. In front of her computer, another team member is designing an online course on global social entrepreneurship whose title dares high school students to *Start Something That Matters*. The team's graphic designer is creating a new website for the second iteration of the TRAI Summit, a two day event that engages students from ASB and Mumbai in finding real solutions for real problems using Technology, Robotics, and Artificial Intelligence. Another member is putting the finishing touches on the PD 3.0 report, the work of a year-long staff task force charged with researching and developing a new model of Professional Development for schools of the future. On the secondary campus the team's director is meeting with the school's Leadership Team and a data scientist to unveil the Learning Analytics system prototype that Re.D Studio has been developing for the last six months. This is only a snapshot of a typical day.

Driven by Impact

In 2011, ASB's Leadership Team created an R&D Staff Team to focus on researching new practices, approaches, and systems for the future of learning at the school. The team was comprised of voluntary faculty members who exhibited a desire to push the boundaries of their own teaching and learning. Working in small faculty task forces, the work of the R&D Staff Team began to have an immediate impact when the school was challenged with contributing to the design of our new elementary school and the redesign of our secondary school. The R&D task force on Facilities Design was able to study how different kinds of learning spaces impacted classroom interactions, student access to learning materials, collaboration and flexible use. A year later our new elementary school and the redesigned Middle and High School learning space were being used for multiple purposes with soft moveable furniture that invited and kindled social and individual learning engagements throughout both campuses. Another important impact of our early R&D work was on our school culture. Suddenly, a high school English teacher from the R&D task force for Blended/Online Learning was developing a new online course, a science teacher who was on the Gamification task force had gamified her high school physics class, and members of the PBL task force were converting their traditional curricular units into Project-Based Learning units in the Middle and Elementary Schools. The learning of the R&D staff team was driving new grassroots practices throughout our school. Two years of the work of an R&D Staff Team were enough to let us know we were onto something big. Since that first year, the R&D Staff Team at ASB has doubled in number. The impact of R&D work and the potential to provide research based innovation and relevant meaningful learning for our students led to the formation of our R&D Department.

R&D: More than a Department - A New Operating System

At its core, R&D at our school is a new operating system for sustaining innovation for relevant student learning. In *Accelerate: Building Agility for a Faster-Moving World*, John Kotter (2014) frames the need for this kind of operating system:

The world is now changing at a rate at which the basic systems, structures, and cultures built over the past century cannot keep up with the demands being placed on them. Incremental adjustments to how you manage and strategize, no matter how clever, are not up to the job. You need something very new to stay ahead in an age of tumultuous change and growing uncertainties. The solution is not to trash what we know and start over but instead to reintroduce, in an organic way, a second system – one which would be familiar to most successful entrepreneurs. The new system adds needed agility and speed while the old one, which keeps running, provides reliability and efficiency (pp. vii-viii).

Our R&D department functions as a flexible, agile operating system focused on researching and developing new practices, approaches, and systems for the future of our school. We do this by networking with many volunteers from across our school. In this way we are able to incorporate diverse perspectives across the school as we research and develop new practices, approaches, and systems for our students while the traditional school operating system implements and embeds new practices that impact our students' learning.

Prototyping, a Core Competency

Michael Schrage wasn't exaggerating when he declared that "Effective prototyping may be the most valuable core competence an innovative organization can hope to have" (Peters, 1987). Prototyping allows us to develop new teaching and learning provisions that are informed and improved to meet the needs of our students in our teaching and learning contexts. We recognize that we have an ethical responsibility to provide thoughtful, high quality learning experiences for our students. Therefore, 'Always-beta' development of our prototypes is a core value and the methodology of our work. 'Always-beta' is a term that comes from the software industry and indicates both a finished product that meets a need but also continues to undergo further development (Hoffman, 2014; Wikipedia, 2013).

Bookmaking for Social Justice - an ES Day 9 Course

Our Day 9 Prototype illustrates how 'always-beta' prototyping enables us to research and develop new provisions that impact student learning while continuing to improve those provisions through further iteration. The prototype began when a group of Elementary School teachers were presented with an open day on the calendar, and a question, "What if you could design a new day of school, what would that look like?" The group identified these three key goals for the new day of school:
- Provide students and teachers with an experience in a day-long project based inquiry.
- Provide a high degree of choice for students *and* teachers.

- Provide students and teachers with an experience of multi-age learning teams.

The team created and ran the initial prototype day. A groundswell of positive response from teachers, students and parents followed. Through two more iterations of Day 9, several aspects of the prototype were improved, resulting in greater student choice, and improved day-long inquiry projects. Months after our final prototype, a new practice based on the prototype called ES Studio became a part of the school week. The success of the ES Day 9 prototype also opened the door to a Day 9 Prototype in our Middle School, around the same basic question, *"What if you could design a new day of school, what would that look like?"* This has evolved into Studio 6. (More on this prototype is shared in the *Accelerating Studio 6* chapter.)

Impacts of R&D Work

Below is a summary of some of our prototypes and their impact on our school and our students.

Exploration/ Prototype	Charge	Impact
Alternative School Year Calendar (2012 - 2013)	Time is one of our most precious and limited resources. Evaluate the use of time in school.	Implemented a research-based calendar to support student learning. Created an Intersession prototype http://www.asbintersessions.org Researched and developed a new model of PD for schools of the future.

Building a Maker Culture (2013 - present)	Explore the Maker Movement and maker culture and how they may support self-directed learning.	Developing insights into how to engage parents and students in growing a maker mindset
		Developing making and tinkering spaces across the school
		Providing Professional learning support to teachers as they explore integration of making into their teaching.
Design Thinking (2013 - present)	As a process for innovation, creating, making, and problem solving, how might Design Thinking impact teaching and learning?	Created ASB's first student led Global Social Entrepreneurship Summit
		Core component of Middle School Day 9 Prototype
Elementary School Day 9 Prototype (2013 - 2014)	What if we created a new day of school for Elementary School Students? (The school has an eight-day schedule; Day 9 was a different day)	K-5 students experienced a high degree of enthusiasm, engagement, and collaboration during learning through day-long inquiry projects.
		Teachers developed professionally around: project-based learning, teaching multi-age groups of

| | | students, leveraging choice to increase motivation for learning

Creation of a Middle School Day 9 Prototype
bit.ly/MSDay9 |
|---|---|---|
| **Middle School Day 9 Prototype or Studio 6 (2013 - present)** | What if we created a new day of school for Middle School Students? | Middle School students ascribed high value to knowledge and skills learned during week-long inquiry projects

Middle School students reported high value of learning through creating and making

Learning value resulted in increased duration of prototype (from 2 days to 1 week) |
| **Library 3.0 (2012)** | There is an ongoing revolution in the ways information is created, shared, and stored. This has disrupted the conception of what a library is. Re-design Library for the future at ASB. | Change in role of the librarian - from curator of books to Information Literacy Coach

Design of library space - comfortable, flexible, and adaptable venues for |

		inviting sustained learning engagement. Moved from moderated access to open access & greatly increased circulation
Mobile Learning (2012 - present)	The growth and potential of the use of mobile devices (such as tablets and smartphones) to support learning cannot be ignored. Study the potential for mobile devices to impact teaching and learning at ASB.	Educators actively and reflectively seeking how best to use mobile devices to support teaching and learning. Developing data visualization tools to better understand impact of mobile devices
Online/Blended Learning (2011 - 2012)	Offerings of online and blended learning courses are increasing at a rapid pace. Investigate how online and blended learning might impact student learning at ASB.	ASB High School Students can choose electives from 40 online courses offered http://www.asbacademy.org Students have access to courses they would not otherwise have access to, e.g. forensic science, entrepreneurship, American sign-language Students are gaining skills for learning

		successfully online.
Parent R&D (2012 - present)	Partnering with parents to "R&D" catalyze relevant teaching and learning approaches, practices, and systems.	Parents are engaged as partners in sustained innovation Parents are engaged as hands-on catalysts for innovative change initiatives Creation of The Parent Learning Academy (PLA) http://www.asbpla.org
Project-Based Learning (2011 - 2014)	Study, prototype, research and create a PBL Model for ASB.	Development of a PBL Model for ASB Developed skill and capacity for teaching PBL at ASB Gathered insight into what catalyzes successful PBL at ASB http://bit.ly/pblreport
R&D Book-sharing (Ongoing)	Operating on the belief that books change minds, lives, organizations, and the world, R&D curates a vast sharing library of texts to inform and inspire.	Sharing hundreds of texts with hundreds of community members based on their interests and pursuits. Contributing to a culture of learning, openness to change,

		and questioning the status quo of school.

How R&D Work Becomes the New Normal

While prototyping gives us valuable on-the-ground context for iterative research and development, decisions about implementation and embedding new practices, approaches or systems belong to our school's Leadership Team. When our research and prototype reports go to the Leadership Team, they decide whether to accept or reject recommendations, put a hold on them, or even send them back to our R&D department for further research and development. One example is the 2011 *R&D Report on Multi-age Classrooms*. The report identified many benefits and recommendations for multi-age classrooms in schools. The Leadership Team decided that the transient nature of our student and teacher populations limited the potential benefits of multi-age classrooms at this point and time, and placed the recommendation 'on hold'. On the other hand, the 2012 *R&D Report on Alternative School Year Calendars* resulted in approved recommendations to:

- balance the school calendar,
- create an engaging Intersession program,
- research and develop a model for the future of professional development for schools.

Intrinsic Motivation = Insourcing Expertise

Our R&D Teams are voluntary teams of faculty, parents, and students. We strive to provide our teams with the conditions of autonomy, competence, and relatedness to others, (identified as essential conditions for intrinsic motivation from a mature theory of human motivation called Self-Determination Theory) in order to foster intrinsic motivation, high quality work, and commitment of our teams over time. We encourage team members to choose to engage based on their personal interests. We support them with resources, and provide time for them to meet to work in teams. This has resulted in more than just research-based practices. It has resulted in new expertise and leadership at our school.

Where other schools may turn to outside consultants to assess, plan, and lead change efforts, we're more often able to engage in these processes by "insourcing" the expertise and leadership capacity developed by R&D volunteers. For example, in the case of prototyping a new Project Based Learning Model across the school, twenty-five staff volunteered to prototype a PBL unit using our new PBL Model. At the end of the prototyping process, we had a rigorously researched and developed PBL model and several colleagues who had insourced expertise and capacity for teaching using a Project-Based Learning approach.

Keys for Successful R&D in Schools

Change always requires a change of status quo thinking. In order to bring something new and impactful to schools, the thinking has to be different. R&D departments or teams must be intentional about reading, learning, thinking, and opening up to new ideas that challenge their own status quo before they can impact the status quo thinking of their colleagues, professional cultures, and the school communities. School leaders must communicate a strong value for innovation and supporting R&D work in school. Changing the status quo operation of your school will cause discomfort and misunderstandings. It will challenge assumptions, existing programs, and even the roles of educators. R&D in schools is always about students. It doesn't matter if you have an R&D department, an R&D team, or a studio. It doesn't matter what books you've read, or what you say. What matters is that you and your team are committed to creating real innovations that make a difference for students.

CHAPTER 3

WHERE DO R&D TOPICS COME FROM?

Where do R&D topics come from? Over the past four years, we've been asked this question a lot by school leaders. School leaders want to understand what kind of decision making process guides our selection of topics to research and develop. This is a fundamental question that we continue to ask in our work. In this chapter we'll share with you four main drivers for choosing topics and a set of 6 plus factors that we use to make choices and decisions for researching and developing the topics in the school divisions, departments, classrooms, and other spaces.

We look to the four main drivers to ensure the topics that we choose are relevant and focused on the needs of our students. These are the drivers:
- Current and emerging global trends
- Major relevance to our school mission and core values
- Significant potential advantage to current teaching and learning
- Sudden urgency to meet unexpected needs

Current and Emerging Global Trends
These are the trends that are currently shaping our world and are predicted to shape our world in the future. We read about these trends from books like *21 Trends for the 21st Century*, reports on global trends from a variety of sources such as the Institute For The Future (IFTF), Gartner and Forrester forecasting companies, and global think-tanks like the Millennium Project and the Organization for Economic Co-operation and Development (OECD).

Major relevance to our school mission and core values
We consider new topics in the context of their potential to have major relevance to the school's ability to achieve its mission.

Significant potential advantage to current teaching and learning

The topic has clear potential to result in creating new innovations with significant advantage over what currently exists.

Sudden urgency to meet unexpected needs

Unpredictable events or new knowledge created, require sudden research and development in order to meet important needs of the school.

These have been the drivers to systematic research and development at ASB from the inception of R&D in 2011 to the present. The example below illustrates how using these drivers systematically drives the relevance of R&D work for our school and our students.

Example: Facilities Design as a Topic for R&D

In the fall of 2011, the purchase of a site to build a new elementary school became increasingly probable. In October the purchase was successful and ASB faced the prospect of designing, constructing, and opening a new elementary school for students in August 2012. ASB would have to work with sudden urgency not just to open a new school building, but a school building that would best serve its students. ASB needed to study 21st century school facilities and design - specifically how school design might support 21st century teaching and learning - and they needed to do it quickly. Global trends were already driving changes in school design around the world. But in our case, the drivers for choosing 21st Century Facilities design were the **sudden urgency to meet the needs of all of our students and the major relevance of 21st century learning spaces to our school mission.**

The R&D team was able to provide fast, focused research to the school's leadership team at a key decision making stage. This led to the creation of 21st century learning spaces that support relevant learning for our students.

New 5th Grade Learning Space in the Elementary School

The table below shows a cross section of R&D topics that we have chosen in the past and the main drivers for their selection.

R&D Topics	Major Drivers For Choosing R&D Topics
Games-Based Learning (2011)	• Significant potential advantage to current teaching and learning
Online Blended Learning (2011)	• Current and emerging global trends
Project Based Learning Task Force (2011)	• Current and emerging global trends • Major relevance to our school mission and core values • Significant potential advantage to current teaching and learning
Mobile Learning (2012)	• Current and emerging global trends
Maker Mindset (2013)	• Current and emerging global trends • Major relevance to our school mission and core values • Significant potential advantage to current teaching and learning
Intersessions Prototype (2013)	• Significant potential advantage to current teaching and learning

	• Major relevance to our school mission and core values
Learning Analytics (2014)	• Current and emerging global trends • Major relevance to our school mission and core values • Significant potential advantage to current teaching and learning
Social Entrepreneurship (2014)	• Current and emerging global trends • Major relevance to our school mission and core values

Once we've identified topics for school research and development, we look at a series of plus factors for successful R&D that help us choose where, when, and how best to bring these new topics down from 30,000 feet to the ground level of our teaching and learning contexts. The presence of clear 'plus' factors at the onset of new R&D work increases the likelihood that new innovation efforts will result in relevant and meaningful impact. A lack of these 'plus' factors increases the likelihood that new innovation efforts will lead to poor results and lost opportunities elsewhere. The table below shows the 6 plus factors we use for engaging in new R&D work.

'Plus' Factors for Engaging in New R&D Work	
Potential Impact *There is a strong perceived advantage between proposed R&D work and what currently exists.*	If this R&D work doesn't have the potential for a significant advantage over what already exists, the work won't have a meaningful impact or return on investment.

Champion Score *The work has an inspired/committed champion who wants to lead this R&D work.*	Inspired committed champions persist through obstacles, increase awareness, and have a vision for high impact. This increases the chances of success and the ultimate quality and impact of R&D work.
Re.D Studio HR Cost *The anticipated human resource cost for the proposed R&D work.*	Committing to work on one topic in a particular division or classroom has a cost. Is the human resource cost worth the potential impact? How does spending HR resources on this new work affect current R&D work?
Degree of Innovation *The anticipated innovation results will be more a new invention than an incremental change.*	Will the R&D work result in bringing something truly new to our school and our students, or will this work be a variation of what already exists for our school and our students?
Receptivity to Innovation *The degree of receptivity to innovation in the proposed innovation context.*	Without receptivity to innovation in a school division, department or classroom, innovation won't be an outcome of R&D efforts and investments.
Synergy *Clear synergies already exist that promise to multiply the impact of an innovation.*	Synergies between different R&D work and new school innovations can create new possibilities, new choices, and new topics. For example, synergies between the Maker Mindset Prototype and Social Entrepreneurship may result in synergy that multiplies the impact of both.

The four main drivers allow us to take a systematic approach to choosing relevant, potentially high-impact topics for R&D at our school. The 6 plus factors allow us to research and develop these new topics in ways that increase the likelihood that R&D work will result in successful innovations that meet our students' needs.

When creating your own school R&D, establishing the drivers for selecting topics is an important step you will want to take early on to ensure your work is relevant and has maximum impact on student learning. Similarly, developing a set of Plus Factors will help you select the most fertile grounds where investment in R&D can lead to developing these topics into real innovations on the ground.

CHAPTER 4

The Dual Operating System

"Knowledge has changed; from categorization and hierarchies, to networks and ecologies. This changes everything and emphasizes the need to change the spaces and structures of our organizations" (Siemens, 2006).

John Kotter's work points to the most essential structure for effective R&D in schools which is a new dual operating system. In schools this new operating system neither sits in isolation, nor is part of the hierarchy of the traditional school operating system. Instead it is a connective parallel operating system that brings a new functionality to the traditional school. This new R&D operating system engages in fast, agile, and focused research and development to sustain innovation for relevant learning.

A Dual Operating System for an organization has two operating systems - a traditional Hierarchy Operating System that operates reliably and efficiently combined with a new operating system, the Network or R&D Operating System that focuses on rapid innovation and operates with speed, agility, and focus. The Hierarchy acts to establish reliability and efficiency by coordinating action and optimizing performance through proven processes. The R&D Operating System provides new capacities for strategic change. It operates with speed, agility, and focus, networking across silos and ranks to engage many people in leading strategic innovation (Kotter, 2012). The result of the Dual Operating System is an organization that is reliable, efficient, *and* fast, agile, and focused to pursue new opportunities and keep pace in a rapidly accelerating change environment.

Hierarchy Operating System	R&D Operating System
• Creates reliability & efficiency • Coordinates action • Optimizes performance Carries out proven processes: • planning • budgeting • measuring • job defining, staffing and training	• Creates speed, agility, and focus to pursue urgent opportunities or dodge threats • Networks across organizational silos & ranks • Engages many people in leading change Provides new capacities for: • gathering information • making decisions • instituting change

(Adapted from Kotter, 2014)

ASB's Dual Operating System was created by the school's Leadership Team in 2011.

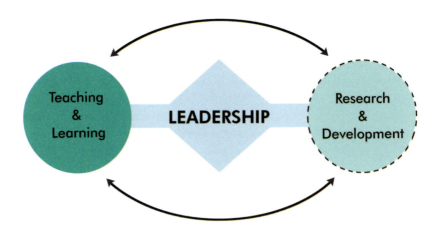

The Hierarchy Operating System

In ASB's dual operating system, the Hierarchy Operating System is a system that educators, parents, and students easily identify. The purposes and functions of this operating system are familiar, accepted, and embedded in our minds. We know why schools exist, what they tend to look like, how they are organized, and how one school is compared with another. This system enables educators to efficiently and reliably meet the needs of students, every day. When this operating system is high functioning, people have shared values, clear understandings, and clear roles and responsibilities. The organizing structure of the Hierarchy Operating System allows people to orchestrate, coordinate, and optimize to achieve results ranging from safety, health, and the cultivation of core values, to the desired results for learning and personal development.

The same roles, structures, processes, and time spent delivering on the promises of the school, preclude the Hierarchy Operating system from having the speed, agility, focus, and knowledge needed in order to keep step with the rapidly accelerating change environment.

The R&D Operating System

The second operating system at our school is our R&D Operating System. In the context of schools, this is an operating system that is nearly completely unknown by educators, parents, or students. The purposes and functions of this operating system are unfamiliar and neither understood nor accepted. In the context of the world's organizations and industries, this second operating system is familiar, understood and accepted. *And* it is disrupting the way the world works. It is the structure of the start-up company. Start-ups are fast, agile, and focused. They are structured and behave like networks - developing and growing nodes of knowledge, skills, and capacities -- they need to take actions. The fast learning, focus and agility of start-ups are the capacities required for success by any organization in an accelerating change environment. These capacities enable startups to out-focus, outlearn, and outmaneuver established hierarchical companies and organizations, including universities and schools.

The efficiency, quality control, and scale capacities that enabled schools and students to thrive in the past are not enough for them to thrive in the future. R&D is the second operating system at our school that explores, studies, prototypes, researches, and scales new teaching and learning approaches, practices, and systems that advance relevant learning in an accelerating change environment. These are core innovation processes used in the context of R&D work.

Interdependence For Innovation In A Dual Operating System

The interdependence of the R&D Operating System and the Hierarchy Operating System is essential to sustain innovation for relevant learning. This interdependence is outlined in the chart below.

Hierarchy Operating System	R&D Operating System
Relies on R&D for research findings, recommendations, and new innovations that meet important learning needs and information that supports their successful implementation. Relies on R&D to provide methodology expertise and facilitation for the most critical innovation teams across the school. Relies on R&D to develop innovation skill capacity throughout the hierarchy by identifying and training personnel on the skills they need to develop in order to drive innovation. Relies on R&D to establish, monitor, and develop Essential	Relies on the Hierarchy leadership team to model interaction with R&D. Relies on the Hierarchy for authentic teaching and learning contexts for prototyping, and access to networking with members across school divisions, departments, and teams within the school. Relies on the Hierarchy to decide which innovations to accept, reject, table, or develop further. Relies on the Hierarchy to establish success criteria, action plans, and a timeframe for successful implementation of a new innovation.

| Conditions for effective R&D in schools.

Relies on R&D to continuously identify best practices for school innovation through scouting, researching methods for generating novel ideas, insights, strategic innovation, and open innovation.	

Putting The Dual Operating System To Work – Intersessions
The following example models the successful work of a dual operating system.

Question - What type of school calendar would best support student learning?
Asking this question in the spring of 2012 led to the creation of an Intersession program designed to stem learning loss and increase the school year to 265 days.

Exploring - Spring 2011
R&D work on the school calendar required time and access to network with the faculty and parent R&D teams. These teams were comprised of members across all three school divisions.

These groups read about alternative school year calendars being used around the world; they created, tinkered with, and shared several alternative school year models and why those models might meet the needs of our school context. Studying alternative year calendars was the outcome of this networked exploring.

Studying & Researching - Fall 2012

A Staff R&D Task Force required time and access to faculty and the parent community in order to study and research what school calendars would best support student learning at ASB.

A key finding of this study was that long school breaks lead to significant learning loss and lost classroom time that is spent re-teaching previously covered concepts. Another finding was that Intersession programs were shown to be effective in stemming learning loss. Additional research and surveying of our own community showed significant faculty and parent interest in alternative school calendars that met students' and educators' needs. Sharing the findings and our recommendations for what school calendar would best support learning at ASB was the final step of this process.

Prototyping - December 2012

The Hierarchy relied on the research findings and recommendations from the *R&D Report on Alternative School Year Calendars* to create a two-year balanced calendar. A second strategic action was to charge R&D with creating a prototype Intersession program to address the problems of learning loss and lost instructional time.

Intersession Prototype - June 2013

R&D created an Intersessions Planning Team to envision and design the Intersession prototype. The first iteration of the prototype ran with a slate of courses across three domains: Mind, Body, and Soul.

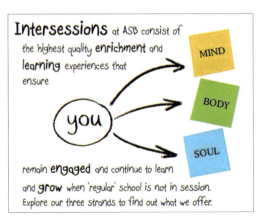

Researching - Enrollment data, parent feedback surveys, student reflections, observational notes, and unsolicited feedback provided strong evidence that the prototype was having a positive impact worth scaling and developing further.

Scaling - Data and insights resulted in making adjustments to the first iteration of the prototype and scaling the summer Intersession by creating fall, winter and spring iterations of the Intersession program. This enabled further refinement based on data and insights for guiding a successful, sustainable Intersession program.

The Hierarchy Operating System relied on R&D for the historical information of the Intersessions prototype and its evolution through different iterations. The Hierarchy also relied on R&D for the instruments for gathering current data, past data, and connection to Intersessions course providers.

In the case of Intersessions, the dual operating system was able to gather and take strategic action, develop a new innovation, refine the innovation, and institute change with great speed at each stage. The end result is an engaging research-based Intersession program that has drawn a total enrolment of nearly 1500 students who have taken over 80 courses in the last 2.5 years, and the option for any student to attend school 265 days a year.

Creating a dual operating system, like all systems that change, is both simple and complex work. During the development of your dual operating system, focus on the vision for bringing sustained innovation for relevant learning to your school. This is crucial. It will help ensure that your dual operating system moves your school past current boundaries and reduces the "I am my position" thinking that can take focus away from the greater purpose of your dual operating system. It's important at some point to finalize your dual operating system so that the stakeholders have clarity about the roles and functions within the new system. As with any innovation effort, expect that things will not be perfect and will require adjustments and iterations to meet the needs of your school. Once an operating system is final, it will be easier to make tweaks and adjustments that are visible. Keeping everyone informed will be important.

Potential Pitfalls for Dual Operating Systems

Factor in Failure - Failure and persistence pave the road to innovation. Your Dual Operating System will experience failures, conflicts, and obstacles. Reserving the space to fail, persist, and make adjustments will improve your system.

Lack of Communication - Your Dual Operating System will ultimately succeed or fail when it succeeds or fails to create a culture for sustained innovation in your school. Lack of communication can be interpreted as a lack of transparency and erode trust in your new system. Or it can be interpreted as a lack of value for the role of innovation at your school. Clear and constant communication can build trust for innovation efforts, communicate the value of innovation, open unexpected channels in the community, and set the stage for participation in innovation efforts.

Attributing personal causes to systems effects - The Dual Operating System will have knock-on effects that can result in people at your school feeling frustrated, displaced, and angry with others even when the issue at hand is an expected result of changes within any organization. Conflicting roles of personnel, conflicting cultural norms, and conflicts around existing programs, schedules and performance expectations are all system conflicts that can be misinterpreted as conflicts with personal causes. Anticipating where and when these conflicts might arise, and framing them and working to address these conflicts as system effects can help strengthen the health and functions of your dual operating system and avoid destructive personal conflict that can damage your operating system.

Lack of Support from Key Players - Commitment to innovation from key players drives community engagement. This opens up spaces for prototyping and other avenues where motivated individuals can engage in R&D work. When there is a lack of support from key players, these spaces, avenues, and intrinsic motivation for R&D work diminish and, in turn may hinder or harm your Dual Operating System. Ensuring that your leadership team and key players share a commitment to innovation and model this commitment will support success of your Dual Operating System.

CHAPTER 5

Essential Conditions for Successful Research and Development in Schools

If change was simply a matter of creating strategy and completing actions, change efforts would be vastly more successful. When Drucker commented that *"Culture eats Strategy for breakfast,"* he was highlighting the role that organizational culture plays in change efforts. In *School Culture Rewired: How to Define, Assess, and Transform,* Gruenert and Whitaker share how culture can be used to support change efforts, and note that culture should be viewed "not as a problem that needs to be solved, but rather a framework that a group can use to solve problems" (2015, p. 6).

We believe that Essential Conditions for R&D in schools can be established and developed to create a culture that drives and fosters successful school change efforts. They are the visible, tangible, describable assets, elements, and capacities for successful strategic research and development in schools. The following eight essential elements enable schools to reliably grow new innovations from *ideas* to *impacts* for sustainable relevant learning.

Empowered Leaders - Leaders are charged and empowered to lead R&D work throughout the school.
- → *Structural Foundation* - A public framework that authorizes, empowers, and defines research and development in education.
- → *Prototyping* – Process for researching and developing new products, practices, approaches, and systems.
- → *Commitment to innovation* - R&D work is authorized and supported by the school.

Engaged Communities - R&D continuously engages and partners with local and global communities.

→ **School Community** - Engages in R&D work within the local community to build a culture of innovation and inform R&D work.

→ **Global Community** - Engages in R&D work beyond the school, developing partnerships and relationships that bring new competencies, opportunities, and context to R&D work.

Intrinsic Motivation - You can't force people to change; you can only help them want to.

→ **Agency** - The ability to shape the work from day to day, make decisions, and act responsibly.

→ **Expertise** - Gaining knowledge and skills.

→ **Connection with peers** - Socially connected work and sharing the work with others.

Future Connection - A relationship with the future exists that guides and compels R&D work today. A future connected school is optimistic, builds pathways, and expects obstacles.

→ **Trends** - Understanding and anticipation of how global trends will impact the practices, approaches, systems, and environments for learning.

→ **Relevant Learning** - Learning that meets important needs that emerge suddenly in an accelerating change environment.

Skill Capacity - Learners, inquirers, and doers are continuously growing, developing, and using their innovation skills.

→ **Recruitment** - identifying, enlisting and recruiting curious self-directed individuals.

→ **Skill Development** - professional learning and applied practice focused on innovation.

Resource Capacity - Resources ensure sustainable inquiries and capacity to act on emerging opportunities.

→ **Budget** - Access to funds for research and development (funding should be a constraint, not a barrier to agile R&D.)

→ **Facilities** - Access to places and spaces for meeting with teams, running prototypes, hosting events, and displaying R&D work.

→ **Materials** - Quick access to basic material and sustainable sourcing practices for specialized materials.

Design Thinking Competence - Design Thinking is embedded as a core process for research, capacity building, and innovation.
→ **Capacity** - Amount of competence and knowledge for design thinking.
→ **Always Beta Culture** - An expectation for developing quality prototypes, that meet teaching and learning needs, with an expectation for ongoing development.

Impact Validity - Valid R&D work is democratically developed, deepens understanding, and provides new answers. It relies on multiple sources, and results in changed practices and beliefs that impact learning.
→ **Democratic** - R&D work that uses multiple perspectives to guide the design of your research, the analysis of your data, and implementation of your actions.
→ **Findings** - R&D work produces new answers and provokes important new questions. They result in changed practices that improve learning.
→ **Data** - R&D work uses multiple sources and types of data to support credible, meaningful conclusions.
→ **Informed Community** - Regular communication of R&D work and its impacts on learning.

Without these Essential Conditions, innovations may sprout up but lack the space, root systems, and attention they require to produce dependable results. Growing and leveraging these conditions results in schools that move from sporadic innovation efforts to systematic research and development. These schools don't depend on irreplaceable innovation leaders. They develop many skilled innovation leaders who lead innovation throughout the school. These schools leverage the conditions to ease innovation instead of accepting barriers to innovation. They create clear pathways for innovation by inviting and facilitating participation in innovation from all stations of their school. Intentionally establishing, using, and growing the Essential Conditions has a multiplier effect that creates new energy and capacity for innovation.

Essential Conditions in 2011

In the fall of 2011, R&D at ASB started with a nine member voluntary Staff R&D Team. We were charged with researching and developing new learning approaches, practices, and systems for the future of ASB. In 2011 we didn't know about Essential Conditions for innovation or how to grow them. We began with our team and our charge. Looking back, here is a look at our Essential Conditions in 2011.

Empowered Leaders was our founding condition. In the spring of 2011, the school Leadership Team took decisive action and created version 1.0 of our Dual Operating System. Our existing hierarchy formed the Hierarchy School Operating System. The new R&D Operating System formed the second system. This decision and action established, authorized, defined, and empowered R&D work at ASB.

Engaged Communities was a pre-existing condition that enabled R&D to begin successfully. A culture of trust in school leadership and a culture of successful technology integration created an atmosphere of positive expectations that permeated the school. Our *Engaged Community* enabled the launch of the R&D Operating System into a supportive change-seeking environment.

Intrinsic Motivation was the first condition that was strategically increased and leveraged by the R&D Operating System in 2011. The nine member Staff R&D Team along with approximately 70 other educators across the school divisions volunteered to explore, study, and research new approaches, practices, and topics. R&D work was intentionally designed and structured on the basis of research on intrinsic motivation and the belief that you can't force

Staff R&D Team considering Implications for ASB

people to change in ways that last. You can only help them want to change.

In 2011 the R&D Operating System grew and leveraged intrinsic motivation by the following main actions.

- Relying on volunteers to choose; personal choice and responsibility provided educators with a high degree of *agency*.
- The knowledge and skills they gained during their exploring, studying, and researching provided educators with growing *expertise*.

Intrinsic Motivation had the effect of driving commitment to R&D work. The Staff R&D Team and their colleagues pushed through obstacles and produced quality work that went beyond our expectations, and in many cases increased interest and investment of time in R&D work throughout the school.

Future Connection was explicit in our charge to create approaches, practices, and systems for the future of our school. It was a frame for R&D Task Force work in 2011. *Future Connection* expanded team members' understanding and use of research. R&D became more active consumers of research in order to explore and study in our task forces, while also becoming active researcher-practitioners. What does the body of research say about Project Based Learning? What does *our* research say about Project Based Learning at ASB? *Future Connection* connected research to our learners and their specific contexts.

Skill Capacity for R&D work in 2011 was a process and a by-product of curious self-directed inquiry. What should our charge sheets look like? How will colleagues lead colleagues in task forces? Where do we find the research resources we need? How do we report our findings and recommendations? At this point in the R&D Operating System's development, learning by doing was the most effective approach to building innovation *Skill Capacity*.

Resource Capacity was a pre-existing condition. The R&D Operating system relied on volunteers. There was no staffing expenditure or stipend for R&D work. *Resource Capacity* enabled us to purchase a wide variety of books from diverse industries, and topics ranging from change management, leadership, neuroscience, emerging technologies, to future trends, innovation, and educational pedagogy. The books supported exploring, studying, and researching of the R&D Task Forces as well as a school wide culture of reading outside of the typical range of professional books. Any person in the school who was interested in a book title we had ordered could have one by signing for it. *Resource Capacity* supported diverse professional reading to fuel an innovation culture. It had the effect of indicating that thinking and dreaming big about the future of the school were realistic, worthwhile pursuits.

Design Thinking Competence never became a condition for R&D in 2011. The primary reason for this was that almost all of our work and time was being spent exploring, studying, and researching. We weren't doing very much prototyping or scaling in this first

Book sharing fuels an innovation culture

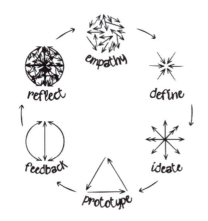

Henry Ford Learning Institute – Design Thinking Model

year. Not until the end of the first year did we have findings and recommendations that we could act on to design and create prototypes. In 2011, the *Design Thinking Competence* that soon became essential in R&D work, didn't exist. We weren't at a place in our development where *Design Thinking Competence* could be an essential condition.

Impact Validity for R&D work was both a condition that we strategically planned for at the start of 2011, and a condition we learned to create out of necessity. The R&D Task Force work was undertaken by many educators across school divisions and facilitated by our Staff R&D Team members.

Democratic Validity was easily achieved by the end of the first year. After agreeing on findings and recommendations as an R&D Staff Team, individual R&D Task Forces presented those findings and recommendations. These were either accepted, rejected, sent back for further work, or tabled by our Leadership Team. Many perspectives informed the work from initial inquiry to the stage of presenting findings and recommendations. This ensured that the work had democratic validity.

Findings Validity was sparked by the task force reports. Not only did the reports result in answers to our initial questions, they also provoked many new questions and insights that rippled throughout the school community and into future R&D work. "Research shows clear benefits with multi-age classrooms. Will multiage classrooms really work at ASB?" "Project Based Learning leads to increased engagement, collaboration, interdisciplinary learning and skill application. Is it compatible with the PYP and the IB?" These were a few examples of the new questions and answers that our *Findings Validity* provoked during the first year.

Informed Community resulted from presenting the work-in-progress to the school's board of trustees, to faculty members and to the international school community during ASB Un-Plugged 2012. We also shared our research findings and recommendations with the school's Leadership Team. Participation by educators across the three school divisions also informed the community. But in 2011, regular communication of R&D work and its impacts on learning didn't occur. We had process work, but there were no innovations that impacted students to share.

Empowered Leaders was our most critical condition for starting the R&D Operating System. This condition established ASB's commitment to school innovation. The Dual Operating System defined the purpose, established a leader, and the space where school R&D work could begin. *Engaged Community* provided an environment of positive expectation for launching the R&D Operating System. *Resource Capacity* allowed us to read widely and dream big. Those three conditions were pre-existing conditions provided by the Hierarchy Operating System. The other conditions could only be created and developed organically by the R&D Operating System as it engaged in school innovation work. *Intrinsic Motivation* was strategically developed but the condition also increased naturally as the Staff R&D Team led their Task Force inquiries.

Skill Capacity was the condition best developed through learning by doing research and development work. The innovation skills the R&D Operating System needed next were the skills needed most during the first year of R&D. *Future Connection* and *Impact Validity* were more than just inert concepts for us in 2011. We had the space, the charge, and the real contexts to practice research and development at our school. We were working toward the future and our students of the future needed our work to be valid.

Essential Conditions for Starting Your R&D Operating System

We believe that *Empowered Leaders* is a prerequisite Essential Condition for your school to establish a commitment to innovation. Other Essential Conditions will pre-exist to varying degrees. These are conditions you can leverage immediately to establish an R&D Operating System. Establishing and growing new Essential Conditions will require you to assess, plan, and take strategic action. Other conditions can only be established as a by-product of school innovation work. Intentionally establishing and growing these conditions is intentionally building a culture for sustaining successful R&D work at your school.

Essential Conditions in 2015

In 2011 the Essential Conditions were our pre-conditions and our urgent needs. We either had them in some measure or we *had* to have them in order to do innovation work. Since then, the R&D Operating System has grown from a Staff Team of 9 voluntary educators to an R&D Department focused on many school innovation efforts while also facilitating Staff, Parent, and Student R&D Teams to lead and participate in school innovation work. In 2015, our focus and use of the Essential Conditions has shifted from developing the existing Conditions or creating them from scratch, to identifying particular Essential Conditions that can be strategically leveraged and bolstered to ensure that specific innovation efforts will have the key conditions that will lead to successful inquiry, prototyping and development. An important step that allowed us to begin leveraging the Essential Conditions was the creation of the Essential Conditions Rubric. The Rubric enabled us to strategically evaluate, plan, and act in order to drive specific innovation efforts and build our innovation culture. It allows us to first, identify key conditions that will likely increase the success of an innovation effort, and then use the rubric to evaluate the Essential Conditions and leverage or bolster them for successful innovation.

The Essential Conditions Rubric below describes what each of the Essential Conditions for Effective R&D would look like at three different stages (Entry, Emerging, Innovation) at a school. A Condition at an Entry level is being planned for or just beginning to support successful innovation in a school. An Emerging condition is supporting successful R&D in multiple spaces and places throughout the school. An Innovation condition has become an embedded part of the school culture that supports innovation as the status quo throughout the school.

Innovation Audit - Essential Conditions for Effective R&D for Schools

R&D in schools is about meeting the needs of learners for relevant learning in a rapidly accelerating change environment. Effective R&D occurs in schools when Essential Conditions are developed to create a culture where sustained innovation becomes the new status quo. Below are Essential Conditions for R&D in schools.

Empowered Leaders - Leaders are charged and empowered to lead R&D work throughout the school.

Entry	Emerging	Innovation
Structural Foundation School leaders discuss possible R&D functions and value in their school.	*Structural Foundation* School leaders have a prototype model for R&D that defines purpose and decision making processes. The school begins developing strategies to introduce R&D prototypes into core hierarchy of the school.	*Structural Foundation* School leaders use and share an effective framework or model that empowers and defines R&D in the school. This framework defines pathways for R&D prototypes to move into day-to-day function of the school.

Prototyping School leaders provide interested individuals with opportunities to explore, experiment, envision, and create models that could transform current practices.	*Prototyping* School leaders are committed to establishing effective prototypes led by volunteers and teams within the school.	*Prototyping* The school is committed to iterating prototypes that work towards meeting school needs for sustainable innovation.
Commitment To Innovation School leaders are open to exploring opportunities for innovation.	*Commitment To Innovation* School leaders promote and support R&D opportunities to innovate student learning. At this stage, the school is exploring ways to integrate R&D work into the core hierarchy.	*Commitment To Innovation* Institutional commitment to R&D and a functioning dual-operating system is in place.

Engaged Communities - R&D continuously engages and partners within the school community and the global* community.

Entry	Emerging	Innovation
School Community Limited opportunities exist for interested community members to engage in R&D work.	*School Community* The school offers opportunities for interested community individuals to participate in R&D work.	*School Community* The school provides a network for interested community members to find, connect, and collaborate with each other on R&D work. R&D work is undertaken by collaborative teams across the school.

Global Community	Global Community	Global Community
The school leaders are considering potential partnerships for R&D work outside the school community.	The school is forming global partnerships to collaborate on R&D work.	R&D work is connected through relationships, partnerships, and participation with the global community. Participation in the global community provides current context and access to expert knowledge, skills, and resources that inform R&D work.

*The community beyond the walls of the school.

Intrinsic Motivation - You can't force people to change, you can only help them want to.

Entry	Emerging	Innovation
Agency The school leaders are exploring ways to provide community members with opportunities to become motivated by their choices, decisions, and responsibilities in R&D work.	**Agency** Community members choose to participate, make decisions, take responsibility, and exhibit energy and interest for R&D work.	**Agency** Voluntary, interest-based teams exist throughout the community. Teams focus on exploring, studying, prototyping, researching, and scaling R&D work. This extends to classroom-based explorations as well.
Expertise The school leaders are exploring ways to provide community members with opportunities to	**Expertise** Participants develop insights, knowledge, and skill that increases their drive to learn more. They rapidly	**Expertise** New expertise and capacity emerge within and from community members. Others recognize R&D

become motivated by developing knowledge and skill in areas of interest.	develop and apply new competencies and knowledge.	participants' expertise and seek to network with them for input, support, new learning, and leadership.
Connection with Peers The school leaders are exploring ways to provide community members with opportunities to become motivated by their connection with peers to do R&D work they value.	***Connection with Peers*** The school provides opportunities for community members to connect with others and network to learn and share R&D work they value.	***Connection with Peers*** R&D participants actively seek to connect with others. They form learning networks to share, co-learn, and co-create.

Future Connection - A relationship with the future exists that guides and compels R&D work today. A future connected school is optimistic, builds pathways, and expects obstacles.

Entry	Emerging	Innovation
Trends Tentative exploration of future trends is taking place. Some of the school leaders are investigating resources and readings about the future.	***Trends*** Global trends are a major influence for most R&D work.	***Trends*** R&D teams understand and anticipate a variety of global trends to explore, study and create new practices, approaches, or systems for learning in the future.
Relevant Learning School leaders consider learners' needs and how they might be met through R&D work.	***Relevant Learning*** The school is aware of the change environment and responds, identifying and prioritizing urgent	***Relevant Learning*** Schools constantly monitor the global change environment, anticipate, and proactively identify new

	learner needs for R&D.	needs and opportunities for highly relevant learning.

Skill Capacity - Learners, inquirers, and doers are continuously growing, developing, and using their innovation skills.

Entry	Emerging	Innovation
Recruitment School leaders consider how they might identify, enlist, and recruit self directed individuals to participate in R&D work.	*Recruitment* The school has identified and enlisted talent that wants to grow their knowledge and innovation skills through R&D work. Developing action plan for recruitment of curious, self-directed individuals.	*Recruitment* Practices are established for identifying and recruiting curious, self-directed talent with a track record of inventing and disrupting the status quo of their own teaching and learning. The school has a dedicated R&D department with full-time staff.
Skill Development Learning opportunities related to R&D work are identified. The school leaders are exploring possible learning opportunities related to R&D work.	*Skill Development* Limited professional learning opportunities and resources related to R&D work are provided by the school for individuals exploring R&D work.	*Skill Development* Systems, courses, professional learning opportunities, and other resources are easily accessible to assist and empower school members to learn and develop their innovation skills.

Resource Capacity - Resources ensure sustainable inquiries and capacity to act on emerging opportunities.

Entry	Emerging	Innovation
Budget School leaders consider how R&D work might be funded.	**Budget** The school provides funding to support R&D work, but constraints limit agility and access to take advantage of emerging opportunities.	**Budget** The school has a sufficient annual R&D budget. Fluid access to funds supports agile R&D. The school employs staff whose role and responsibilities are to lead and engage in R&D work.
Facilities School leaders consider what spaces might be needed for R&D work.	**Facilities** The school allocates space where individuals can do R&D work or host R&D events.	**Facilities** Dedicated spaces exist as a home base for R&D work. Access to places to run prototypes, host events, and display R&D work are provided.
Materials School leaders consider what materials might be needed to begin R&D work.	**Materials** The school has the knowledge of sources to purchase essential materials, storage solutions, and simple purchasing procedures in place.	**Materials** Efficient inventory and storage systems make finding, using, and replacing materials sustainable.

Design Thinking Competence - Design Thinking is embedded as a core process for research, capacity building, and innovation.

Entry	Emerging	Innovation
Capacity School leaders identify and explore design thinking as a key competence in R&D work.	*Capacity* R&D members and individuals, scattered across the school, use design thinking to solve challenging problems and meet authentic user needs. Some individuals have developed skills in facilitating design thinking processes.	*Capacity* Design thinking processes are in constant use across the school to solve difficult problems and systematically research and develop new prototypes that meet learner needs. Many individuals and groups are highly skilled at facilitating design thinking.
Always Beta Culture School leaders give careful thought and consideration to prototype design in order to meet user needs.	*Always Beta Culture* Groups and individuals, scattered across the school, understand that prototypes are never finished and require continued development. Evidence is gathered that can be used to improve prototypes.	*Always Beta Culture* R&D prototypes are adjusted immediately based on evidence. The school continuously improves upon all prototypes.

Impact Validity - Valid R&D work is democratically developed, deepens understanding, and provides new answers. It relies on multiple sources and results in changed practices and beliefs that impact learning.

Entry	Emerging	Innovation
Democratic School leaders support a few interested individuals to collaborate and share their vision of R&D work. R&D decisions are solely made by involved individuals, usually school leaders.	*Democratic* The school supports R&D work done collaboratively and uses perspectives from R&D members and research to inform the process. R&D decisions are solely made by R&D members and school leadership.	*Democratic* R&D work uses multiple perspectives across the school to guide the design of research, analysis of data, and implementation. R&D decisions are presented to the school and any interested individuals may submit input.
Findings School leaders identify questions that can be addressed through R&D work.	*Findings* R&D findings disrupt assumptions, lead to answers, and provokes important new questions related to current practices.	*Findings* R&D findings produce answers that lead to new questions. It deepens and extends understanding. The school has transformed practices based on R&D findings to impact learning.
Data School leaders have identified data that could be collected to see effects of R&D work on student learning.	*Data* R&D members design instruments to measure learner needs and prototype results. The school begins data analysis for relevance and impact on learning.	*Data* R&D teams regularly use multiple sources and types of data to support credible, meaningful conclusions about learner success. New ideas on data collection are being generated and tested regularly.

Informed Community	Informed Community	Informed Community
School leaders consider how they might communicate about R&D work and its effects on learner success.	R&D work updates are shared regularly with the school community.	R&D teams regularly communicate about R&D work and its impact on learning to the school and global community.

Consider This

Which Essential Conditions already exist as assets at your school? What's the most important condition you would need to grow in order for the innovation engine to succeed?

CHAPTER 6

PROTOTYPING IN SCHOOLS

"Effective prototyping may be the most valuable core competence an innovative organization can hope to have."
- Michael Schrage, MIT innovation expert and thought leader

"An R&D department in a school? What do you do?" This is a common refrain in conversations with new acquaintances as well as our friends, families, and colleagues. To those familiar with schools, it is easy to visualize and conceptualize what people working in an athletic department, a finance department, or a mathematics department do every day and why they are doing it. But what does an R&D department do in a school? For those of us who answer this question on a regular basis, if we had to answer with just one word, that word would be Prototyping. It has become the most valuable competency of our R&D department.

Prototyping at ASB
A prototype is an original or first model of something from which other forms are copied or developed. It serves as a first or early example that is used as a model for what comes later. It is putting these model prototypes into real contexts with real people to gather real information quickly (Peters, 1987). Prototyping in schools leads to understandings, insights, and changes that can be acted on to develop and optimize new approaches, practices, or systems that meet the needs of teachers and students in the context of *our* school. The table below shows the differences between piloting and prototyping in schools.

Piloting Vs. Prototyping
Prototyping is an iterative learning, designing, and tailoring process where new practices, approaches, or systems are researched, developed, and tailored to meet learning needs in specific contexts for specific users. On the other hand, piloting is a process of selecting and assimilating a pre-existing practice, approach, or system that claims to meet learning needs in all or most

schools. Piloting is a one time process that stops. Prototyping is an iterative loop of informed decision making that drives continuous development and improvement of new processes, products, or systems for the learners they were designed for.

Piloting	Prototyping
• one iteration • summative • actions taken focus on changing in order to accommodate a new practice • decisions are final	• several iterations • formative & summative • actions taken focus on changing the new practice to accommodate learning • decisions create a loop • decisions → new information → continued development → new decisions

Always Beta Prototyping

"The Hacker Way is an approach to building that involves continuous improvement and iteration. Hackers believe that something can always be better, and that nothing is ever complete." – Mark Zuckerberg (bit.ly/thehackerway)

Schools have an ethical responsibility to provide thoughtful, high quality learning for students. A less-than-quality prototype that has a negative impact on students is not an option in schools. This is why 'always beta' prototyping is a vital methodology that ensures ethical prototyping in schools. 'Always-beta' development is a term that comes from the software industry and indicates both a finished product and a product that is under construction (Wikipedia, 2013). The product is "complete" but there is a promise of continued development. In schools, 'always beta' prototypes must have the quality of a finished program or practice, as well as the expectation that the prototype will continue to develop, deepen, and evolve (Hoffman, 2014).

Further supporting prototyping as an ethical practice in schools is John Hattie's research linking innovative efforts to achievement; *"...a constant and deliberate attempt to improve the quality of learning on behalf of the system, principal and teacher typically relates to improved achievement. The implementation of innovations probably captures the enthusiasm of the teacher implementing the innovation and the excitement of the students attempting something innovative. Often this has been explained as an experimental artifact in terms of a Hawthorne effect. No matter the reason, it appears that innovation per se can have positive effects on students' achievement. Teachers who constantly question "How am I doing", who wish to verify that their methods are having impacts on student learning are the prerequisites for excellence."* (Hattie, 1999, p. 9)

Global Social Entrepreneurship at ASB is an example of an ethical prototyping process. After exploring and studying social entrepreneurship in the fall of 2013, a prototype was  created. The Global Social Entrepreneurship Summit (GSES) prototype was designed to support ASB high school students co-leading and co-facilitating the Summit. Detailed planning and learning were required in order to take the Summit from a concept to an 'always beta' prototyping stage where the R&D department and the students could lead and facilitate the Summit. Thirty three students from nine schools around the world succeeded in learning about the social entrepreneurship model, a model which included designing a social business, creating a business plan, and creating a media marketing pitch for their enterprise.

The GSES prototyping process is allowing us to:
- Develop, test, refine, and iterate methods for teaching students about global social entrepreneurship.
- Develop, test, refine, and iterate methods for teaching students about design thinking.
- Develop our capacity to know what works and what doesn't work in providing a meaningful context for practicing global social entrepreneurship.

- Develop insights for how this prototype might be scaled, modified, or applied in a different learning context such as a classroom.

This deliberate learning and development has required only *one* day of instructional time for eight student leaders. By starting small and learning through iteration, we have insourced knowledge and the insight we need to create a rigorously developed, 'always-beta' prototype that can be ethically scaled and applied in different student learning contexts.

Five Phases for Prototyping

In our work, we've identified five kinds of actions or phases of prototyping. The phases are Exploring, Studying, Prototyping, Researching and Scaling.

An example of prototyping through these phases at ASB is the Internships program (bit.ly/internshipsprogram).

Exploring - The R&D task force first read about Internships across a selection of texts and sources. They began an exploration of internship programs at other schools and universities. Learning during this phase often included expanding knowledge of the scope and variation of practices, and becoming aware of key practices, practitioners, and resources.

Studying - The task force studied a variety of literature on the impact of internships, contacted schools with similar aims and intentions for internships, and also examined public documents of other schools and districts that were offering a broad range of internships. Next the task force shared its findings and recommendations, including the recommendation to create an Internships prototype, and the key considerations for the prototype in the context of ASB.

Prototyping - The R&D task force designed an Internship prototype. The first cohort included 12 students who participated in summer internships. Students and partner organizations provided daily feedback and students received evaluative feedback.

Researching - The feedback gathered by the task force resulted in an important insight: Students who worked on projects *they* viewed as important to the employers, experienced greater satisfaction over the course of their internship.

Scaling - Feedback from the first iteration was used to make changes to the second iteration. The second iteration aimed to increase the likelihood that students would be doing work they viewed as important during the Internship. This iteration of the internship prototype was scaled to serve over 20 students

and included introducing Service Learning Internships and Internships within ASB as two additional types of internships. Currently we're still gathering data and feedback and using it to further develop and expand the Internships program.

Learning Through Prototyping in School

Learning from prototypes is essential for sustainable innovation in schools. Developing prototypes that meet real needs for teaching and learning over time requires a mindset that places a high value on what is often misattributed as failure. The quote *"I have not failed. I've just found 10,000 ways that won't work",* attributed to Edison, illustrates that Prototyping is a rigorous process for bringing new innovations to school. School prototypers must view failure as informative grounds. In this Harvard Business Review article (bit.ly/harvardbusinessreview), Barthelemy & Dalmagne-Rouge make a case for lingering in what they call the "problem space" during prototyping. They make the case that lingering in the problem space helps prototypers push past psychological limits and assumptions, in order to cause a deeper consideration of the problem that can lead to breakthrough insight and innovation (Barthelemy & Dalmagne-Rouge, 2013). Here are some other ways we are learning through prototypes:

- **We are learning how to meet the needs of real students in real contexts** – During our Day 9 Prototype (bit.ly/ASBFF2013) we created a new school day in the Elementary School where students learned through day long projects in multi-age groups. The first prototype was about designing a new day and learning the prototype in a real contexts. The following two iterations were about paying close attention to the elements we were focusing on developing, gathering feedback from users, and making changes to continuously improve the new day.

Day 9 Students participate in an art course

- **We are learning from failures and mistakes** - During the course of a 5th grade homework prototype, we learned that the prototype required more clarity and communication in order to catalyze smooth successful student engagement at home.

- **We are learning how prototypes interact with and impact the status quo** - The Intersessions Prototype (bit.ly/asbintersessions) was designed to keep students engaged and learning during school breaks based on research about learning loss. As courses in programming, project-based design thinking, and making have become successful, their success has impacted our thinking. Should programming be offered more widely? If so, how? How might project-based design thinking courses be used to foster interdisciplinary learning?

- **Gaining insights about what catalyzes or inhibits prototypes** - The iterative nature of prototyping makes it easier to notice the factors and practices that contribute to the success of a prototype as well as the factors and practices that are detrimental to the success of a prototype. Knowing what catalyzes and inhibits practices like Project-Based Learning, for example, results in important insights that can be used to plan successful school wide implementation.

Discomfort of Prototyping

Lingering in the problem space isn't the only uncomfortable aspect of prototyping. Prototyping is an uncomfortable process for any organization. Worthwhile prototypes challenge assumptions and constraints of established practice such as:

- time constraints or schedule structures
- space constraints and usage patterns
- existing programs
- cultural norms
- established roles of personnel

Establishing prototyping as a core competence for innovation, requires more than creating a research and development department or team. It requires school wide value for innovation, understanding of innovation processes, and that the bumps and disruptions are worthwhile discomforts in pursuit of relevant student learning and success.

Consider This

You are planning the first prototype process at your school. How will you prepare for that first prototyping process in order to ensure its success?

CHAPTER 7

Accelerators for School R&D Work

Successful school innovation ultimately boils down to the creation of new practices, approaches, and systems that have a clear and sustainable impact for learners and learning. The evaluation of the Essential Conditions provides the foundation for planning the prototypes of these practices. The eight Accelerators for R&D are used to strategically plan, manage, and evaluate individual prototypes. These are adapted from John Kotter's work. The Essential Conditions need to be leveraged to enable Accelerators to produce lasting school innovations. In order to leverage the Conditions for individual prototypes, it is important to understand Kotter's eight Accelerators.

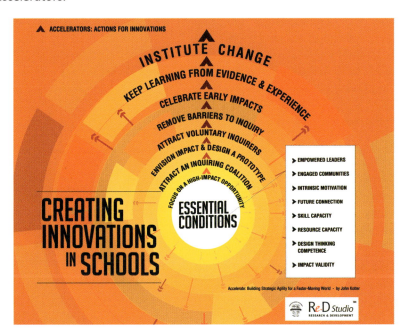

Putting it together - Essential Conditions power the Accelerators

Each Accelerator is a distinct stage for planning and taking action to create prototypes. The eight Accelerators provide crucial action stages for creating successful school innovations from identifying the high-impact opportunity that sparks a new prototype, to instituting a successful prototype as part of everyday practice and culture of a school.

Accelerator 1: Focus on a high-impact opportunity

High-impact opportunities for school R&D have the potential to meet important learning needs. These needs may be driven or influenced by global and societal trends, or by creating significant improvements to existing teaching and learning practices through new innovations in professional learning and technology integration. Another driver for a high-impact opportunity is a school's mission and the core values designed to meet the needs of learners. An example of a high-impact opportunity in our context was the need to *"Provide the highest quality enrichment and learning experiences that stem learning loss when regular school is not in session."* This was the rationale for researching and developing ASB's Intersession Program. Students' needs and our school's mission were the primary drivers that led to creating this new school innovation. Identifying the high-impact opportunity establishes the purpose of specific R&D work and builds understanding and momentum for action.

Accelerator 2: Attract and maintain an Inquiring Coalition

The Inquiring Coalition is a group of people with a shared interest, curiosity, or desire to pursue the high-impact opportunity. The Inquiring Coalition requires a diversity of viewpoints, a collective hunger to learn, and an openness to creating novel ways to meet learning needs. Finally an Inquiring Coalition requires autonomy, responsibility, and resource support. With these traits and conditions, the Inquiring

The Accelerators – Adapted from John Kotter (2014)

Coalition has what it needs to accelerate inquiry into a high-impact opportunity.

Accelerator 3: Envision impact and design a prototype

The primary method for creating high impact innovations for schools is prototyping a new innovation in an authentic context. During this stage, the Inquiring Coalition works to envision the impact of the inquiry, create a prototype, and design or select the strategic actions required to achieve the vision of the prototype. Before envisioning impact and designing a prototype, the Inquiring Coalition may need to build shared understanding through:

- Exploring global trends and current practices
- Studying existing research literature (if there is any)
- Connecting with other organizations or experts
- Using a design thinking process
- Conducting primary research through methods such as interviews, surveys, and focus groups.

Shared understanding creates a starting point for envisioning impact, designing a prototype, and planning strategic actions to research and develop a new practice with speed, agility, and focus for the users that it is intended to impact.

Accelerator 4: Attract voluntary inquirers

A concrete vision and a prototype bring a high impact opportunity from the idea or concept space into the learning space. This attracts voluntary inquirers who can participate in researching and developing the new prototype. Engaging volunteers in prototyping creates ownership, new knowledge, and feedback for improving prototypes and momentum toward creating the vision for impact on learning. These volunteers don't enlist to carry out orders. They join out of a desire to participate in the vision and in creating results that matter and have a significant impact. During this stage, volunteers agree to participate in prototypes, gather and share information, and give timely feedback that can be used to gain insights and accelerate development of a prototype.

Accelerator 5: Accelerate by removing barriers to inquiry

"To intervene means to take action to change what is happening or might happen to prevent counterproductive behaviors and increase group productivity and learning" (Garmston and Zimmerman, 2013, p. 3).

Failure to intercede and remove barriers to inquiry is the kiss of death to R&D work in schools, resulting in failure without learning and loss of credibility and potency for driving change. Prototypes that make an impact will always spark new learning, new energy, new activity, and new communication. New vision and new impacts expose and invite barriers and resistance. Barriers often result from fixed mindsets, existing systems and structures, or key players who actively thwart or fail to support change efforts. Expecting and removing these barriers is essential in order to maintain the energy and momentum of the volunteer inquirers, and to continue gaining insights and making adjustments that increase the impact of a prototype. Removing barriers also provides important insights for scaling or ultimately implementing a prototype in other school contexts.

Accelerator 6: Generate and celebrate early impacts

Generating and celebrating early impacts accelerates the momentum of a prototype. Psychologically, celebrating short term wins energizes the volunteer inquirers, increases understanding, and draws interest and cooperation from others throughout the school. Early impacts also serve as early indicators that the vision and the prototyping process will lead to important impacts for learners.

Accelerator 7: Keep learning from evidence and experience

Early success in researching and developing new prototypes can result in taking your foot off the accelerator before the prototype has reached its desired destination. What is the evidence that a prototype truly has significant impact? What can be improved? What are we learning from prototyping? What new adjustments, alterations, or iterations can we use to realize or expand our original vision? How will we analyze and communicate evidence and information from our inquiry to finalize the research and development of this new innovation for successful implementation in the school?

Accelerator 8: Institute Change

Proposed school innovations are ultimately instituted by a school's Leadership Team. A prototype eventually reaches a decision stage where it is accepted, rejected, put on hold, or it returns to the R&D Operating System for further research and development. When a prototype is accepted, it becomes an innovation to be embedded in school. The Hierarchy Operating System leads and manages the new innovation, so that it becomes effectively and reliably instituted to meet learning needs.

According to organizational change expert John Kotter, 7 out of 10 change efforts fail (HBR, 2012). Good ideas don't translate to good results as often as we anticipate. In *The Innovator's Hypothesis,* Michael Schrage adds that "Implementation frictions typically burn out and blister the inspiration of ideas. Confronting, seducing, and overcoming the coefficients of implementation friction pose the real innovator's dilemma" (Schrage, 2014, p. 28).

The Accelerators for School R&D Work are designed to enable schools to inquire into high-impact opportunities through successful prototyping in the high-friction work of converting inquiries into innovations. In the next five chapters that follow you will read about how we have used the Accelerators to lead and manage several individual prototypes at various stages of development. From chapter to chapter, you will see how these different prototypes with their differing origins, drivers, inquiring coalitions, voluntary armies, and barriers to inquiry, can be led and managed using these Accelerators.

CHAPTER 8

ACCELERATING INTERSESSIONS: ACTIONS FOR INNOVATION

Any time an organization brings wanted change to life, it is important to understand both how that change came to be and how the change might have a lasting impact. At ASB one such change has been the Intersessions program. The program consists of high quality enrichment and learning experiences that ensure students remain engaged and continue to learn and grow when 'regular' school is not in session.

The Intersessions program began as a prototype in the Summer of 2013. The program was developed on the basis of findings from our *2012 R&D Report on Alternative School Year Calendars* (bit.ly/AlternativeSYC) that indicated that learning loss and additional time re-teaching resulted when students spent extended time away from school. The program offered courses that ranged in duration from two to three to six hours

Students on their experience trip during the Photography Intersession course

a day over a period of one to two weeks. Hands-on-learning and interdisciplinary learning were also important elements for the design of Intersessions courses. Equally important was providing a balanced learning program where there were opportunities to learn across three different domains - Mind, Body, and Soul. Below you'll find the complete listing of courses that were provided during the 18 month prototype (January 2013 to September 2014).

Elementary Course Offerings

Body	Mind	Soul
Xsports Mini Tennis	Adventures in Game Design	Dance Drama Damaru
Terrific Tumblers and Magical Maestros	CSI Forensics - Basic level	Look Out World! Here I Come!
Xsports Soccer Tots	Robotics using Lego Mindstorms	Music in Measures
Xsports Basketball	CSI Forensics - Advanced level	
Xsports Table Tennis	Weebot Robotics	
Xsports Tennis	Game Development Quest	
Xsports Indoor Soccer	Programming Magic Club	
Swimming - Flippa Ball	Arduino: Circuits, Engineering, and Computer Programming	
Swimtastic	EAL Bridge Program	
Kid Fit		
Xsport Tri-Golf		
Xsport Soccer		
Xsport Advanced Table Tennis		
Funino Soccer		
Aqua Seals		
Wall Climbing		
Xsport Advanced Soccer		
Aqua Starfish		
Cricket Coaching		
Football - Girls		

Students participating in Xsport Tri-Golf intersession course

Middle/High School Course Offerings

Body	Mind	Soul
Xsports Basketball	Adventures in Game	Fun Science: Energy
Xsports Table Tennis	Design	Mania
Swimtastic	CSI Forensics - Basic	Phun with Physics
Xsports Tennis	level	NuVu Brainwave Art &
Xsports Indoor Soccer	Robotics using Lego	Music
Swimming - Flippa Ball	Mindstorms	NuVu Dancing Robots
Xsport Advanced	CSI Forensics -	NuVu Interactive
Soccer	Advanced level	Storybook
Wall Climbing	Weebot Robotics	NuVu Musical Games
Aqua Dolphins	Dance Drama	Filmmaking: Short
Contemporary Kalari	Senet Game Design	Documentary Films
(Martial Arts)	Game Design for	Wearable Electronics
Funino Soccer	Apple® iOS® &	& Fashion
Xsport Advanced	Android™ with Unity	Photography: The Art
Tennis	Minecraft – Game	of Storytelling
Xsport Advanced	Modding and Java	Dance and Drama
Soccer	Coding	Director's Chair:
Cricket Coaching		Lights! Cameras!

Sailing	College Admissions	Creativity Comes
Rhythmic Dance Forms	Boot Camp	ALIVE!
	Arduino: Circuits,	Nomadic Architecture
	Engineering, and	The Ultimate Chart
	Computer	Buster!
	Programming	The Ultimate DJ
	Global Leadership	The Ultimate Rock Star
	Lab	Theatrics: Make a Play
	Programming Magic	Visual Narratives in
	Club	Film and Photography
	Android App	Paint And Draw Like
	Development	Paul Klee and Others
	Game Development	
	with Unity I: Editor	
	EAL Bridge Program	
	Entrepreneurship	
	Picture Perfect -	
	Portrait Retouching	

Students tinkering with the Arduino circuit board in their Arduino: Circuits, Engineering, and Computer Programming Intersession course

Accelerating Innovation

Intersessions is an example of an innovation that has been successful over time. The program has become part of our ASB students' and parents' plans during the school breaks. Feedback from parents indicates that students would rather attend Intersessions courses than travel. Intersessions is expanding the audience it caters to by opening some of the courses to students outside of ASB. So what were the building stages for Intersessions? Below we look back at the Intersessions Prototype through the lens of the Accelerators in order to understand how the prototype was envisioned, created, executed, and made sustainable.

The Accelerators – Adapted from John Kotter (2014)

Accelerator 1: Focus on a high impact opportunity

During this stage of development, the findings and recommendations from the *R&D Report on Alternative School Year Calendars* served to create the sense of urgency for designing and prototyping Intersessions. The research on learning loss, time spent re-teaching, and particular impact on students whose primary language was not English, created the opportunity to develop the Intersessions Prototype. This report catalyzed important conversations and initial thinking that resulted in the formation of our Inquiring Coalition. (You can read the report here - bit.ly/balancedreport)

Accelerator 2: Attract and maintain an Inquiring Coalition for Intersessions

During this stage we created an Intersessions Planning Team to envision and design the first Intersessions starting in the summer of 2013. This team was formed and charged with creating and executing the Intersession prototype.

Accelerator 3: Envision impact and design a prototype

The Inquiring Coalition began formulating a strategic vision and action plans that would set the prototype in motion. The result was a focus on creating a slate of courses across the three domains of Mind, Body, and Soul as well as key decisions about the design of the courses and who would provide them. Courses would be run by expert coaches and instructors that do not currently teach at ASB or perhaps even teach in schools. Recruiting subject-area experts and coaches and forming those relationships and partnerships were a core part of the vision for the Intersessions prototype.

We prototyped through the following Intersessions after a successful six week summer 2013 prototype:
- Winter 2014
- Spring 1 2014
- Spring 2 2014
- Summer 2014
- Fall 2014

We also prototyped different types of Intersession programs that addressed various student needs that were arising:
- Intersessions Bridge Program
- Intersessions Connect Program

Accelerator 4: Attract volunteer inquirers

The Intersessions Planning Team were our volunteers. They envisioned, designed and planned the prototype. This coalition set to work creating and executing the action plans, building partnerships for designing courses, recruiting instructors, creating schedules, creating communication channels, providing a wide range of material and logistical support, gathering feedback and continually refining the prototype. This resulted in a high level of student and parent engagement, positive feedback and buy-in.

Kid Fit, a course that we prototyped during Winter 2014 Intersession

Accelerator 5: Accelerate by removing barriers to inquiry
We acted to remove barriers. The first barrier was encountered just before the first Intersession. Parents registered their students several weeks in advance. However, the Planning Team noticed a level of uncertainty amongst parents around participation of their children in the program. The Team realized that this uncertainty could become a barrier to the prototype's success.

They acted to remove this barrier by communicating about:
- Transportation - facilitating transportation for students
- Meal information - customizing snacks and lunches for students
- Individualized course schedules

The next barrier that presented itself during the first prototype emerged in the form of an early monsoon. All sports courses were scheduled to run on our outdoor fields and playgrounds. In order to ensure these courses could run, we remodeled our basement levels and created indoor soccer and tennis courts. Our first Intersessions prototype occurred during the monsoons and all our sessions ran smoothly indoors.

The prototyping process uncovered many barriers, some bigger than others. But taking an active stance to identify and remove these barriers throughout each different Intersession allowed barriers to become a basis for improving the quality of the overall program.

Accelerator 6: Generate and celebrate early impacts
Some of the most immediate celebrations for the team was parent feedback. Here are a few examples:

- "I learned that even young children can be taught to be observant, alert and basically to be an investigator."- Grade 2, CSI Forensics
- "My child declared, at the end of the week, that she wanted to direct and produce film for a career. She will be able to transfer the knowledge and skills that she learned in the course to her own video making from now on." - Grade 7, The Producers
- "Creating a business model was a first for my child. She gained significant knowledge of how a company operates. I was happily surprised to see that she extended her interest horizon with an open mind and gained business knowledge at such a young age." - Grade 9, Entrepreneurship

This parent feedback, the daily blog posts on the courses, and a short film created by students during a film making Intersession course - all served as small wins.

Accelerator 7: Keep learning from evidence and experience
This was the final stage of Intersessions for the R&D department. The Intersession program was moving out of prototyping into an established practice at ASB. Our responsibility at this stage is to ensure that the school is equipped with the knowledge, processes, systems, and skilled personnel ensuring sustainable success and continued development of the prototype. For Intersessions that has meant:

- Hire, develop, and empower teams
- Explore ways to sustain student engagement and interest between Intersessions

Accelerator 8: Institute change
The last stage of the Accelerators is institutionalizing Intersessions into the DNA of the school. We believe that this process will occur over time, as the

prototype continues to develop and grow. The R&D department will continue to explore and prototype interesting courses and form new partnerships with experts in various fields, bringing those to the Intersessions Team to execute. We've been ideating further to see what Intersessions could potentially become. Could this be a space for students to travel to places to learn and experience different cultures? How do we leverage the talent of current ASB faculty and staff? These are a few questions that we continue to ask ourselves today. But, Intersessions as a program has run through its prototyping cycle and is on its way to becoming integrated into the culture of ASB.

CHAPTER 9

Accelerating Maker

The Maker Movement is a growing global Do-It-Yourself (DIY) culture. Creativity, collaboration, open access and learning through hands-on learning are hallmarks of the Maker Movement. Starting in the fall of 2013, ASB began exploring making and tinkering as a constructive connective approach to learning with rapidly increasing real-world utility and application. The Maker Mindset Prototype is the name we have given to this overall inquiry. This overarching prototype includes several smaller prototypes that have been designed and developed to inquire into the high-impact opportunity of developing a Maker Mindset for teaching and learning.

Accelerating 1: Focus on a high-impact opportunity
Global trends are driving the global maker movement. The Institute For The Future identifies major drivers of the global maker movement as increasing access to tools, the emergence of open-source software, the blurring of lines between professional and amateur makers, social platforms for collaboration and problem solving, the increasing importance of ecological sustainability, and a quest for authenticity (IFTF, 2008).

At the same time these and other trends are melding and driving the transformation of schooling. For example, in *21 Trends for the 21st Century: Out of the Trenches and into the Future,* Marx (2014) identifies the increasing need for ingenuity as an emerging trend for schools. This trend signals a shift from knowledge acquisition in

Elementary students using an Arduino board to program a fan

siloed classes to knowledge acquisition across disciplines with a focus on constructing new knowledge, generate breakthrough thinking, and creating innovations (Marx, 2014).

The global trends, the high value our school mission places on inspiring continuous inquiry, and capitalizing on internal motivation for learning, were the drivers of our decision to inquire into the opportunity of learning through making and tinkering.

Accelerator 2: Attract and maintain an inquiring coalition

The R&D department acted as the Inquiring Coalition for this prototype.

This core group began reading about the maker movement, reading about the trends that were driving the global maker movement, and talking, thinking, meeting with each other, and tapping into members of the community with a background in making to understand more about it. At the same time the

Parents participate in hands-on making and prototyping

Inquiring Coalition began ordering books, tools, and making materials and learning about making and tinkering first-hand. Soon workspaces became

Staff R&D team members making with Little Bits

cluttered with books about making, microcontrollers, wires, cardboard, and other making materials. Projects like the tissue box guitar, a half-finished drone, several 3D Printing projects, and LED light projects allowed the Inquiring Coalition to learn about making through doing.

Next, the Inquiring Coalition worked with the Parent R&D Team to share information about the global Maker

Movement and learning through making. Based on their new learning, the Parent R&D Team generated implications of learning through making and tinkering for *their* children as well as the implications of learning through making and tinkering at ASB. They repeated this activity with interested faculty and members of the Staff R&D Team. Working with these teams, the Inquiring Coalition was able to grow and expand a palette of ideas, visions, understandings, and insights about where, when, and how to accelerate a Maker Mindset at ASB.

Accelerator 3: Envision impact and design a prototype

Next, the Inquiring Coalition began designing and selecting new strategic actions for learning about making and tinkering while accelerating a maker mindset at ASB. We engaged consultant Gary Stager and NuVu Studios to run workshops for the Parent R&D team and other interested parents in our community. This developed initial awareness, experience, and understanding about making through learning in the school community. The next strategic action was to develop Maker Saturday at ASB to capitalize on the desire our Parent R&D Team had for seeing *their* children learn through making and tinkering. Parent R&D members studied the trends and drivers of the global maker movement. They had also thought deeply about the implications that learning through making might have for their children and for the school. These parents were the early adopters that brought their children to the first Maker Saturdays to learn through making with their children. In a matter of months, Maker Saturdays gained popularity and became a visible evolving event where many students and parents (mostly from the elementary school) were learning through making.

Making using electronics and programing during Maker Saturday

At the same time the Inquiring Coalition collaborated with the Middle School to create a prototype where students would spend two days engaging in projects that relied heavily on learning through making and tinkering, and with the High School by facilitating Maker Challenges. In addition to these strategic initiatives, the Coalition designed and selected many other strategic initiatives. Some of these initiatives were designed prior to engaging volunteer inquirers. Other initiatives emerged as opportunities presented themselves or as volunteers themselves participated in the change vision for making and tinkering. The following are other initiatives that were designed to accelerate a maker mindset.

Maker Prototype Initiatives
STEM Initiative

Programming - opportunities to learn programming during Maker Saturday Engineering Club - a faculty led club

Developing Maker Spaces - creating and provisioning maker spaces throughout the school

Students thinking through solutions at TRAI

Technology Robotics and Artificial Intelligence Summit (TRAI) - two day student summit focused on learning using technology, robotics and artificial intelligence to address real-world challenges

ASB Intersession Courses - offering courses that engaged students in hands-on learning through making and tinkering.

Maker Mornings - opportunities for elementary school students to learn through making and design thinking in the mornings prior to the start of school.

High School Maker Courses - elective courses designed to integrate and develop programming, electronics, design thinking and making knowledge and skills.

Community Access to Materials - offering popular making materials for sale at cost in the school store. South Asian International School Association (SAISA) New Media in Art - Student Conference

Elementary School Faculty Professional Development - PD focused on assessing learning through making and providing practices that support learning through making.

Accelerator 4: Attract volunteer inquirers
The Inquiring Coalition started small by sharing books and making materials with interested teachers and engaging those teachers in conversations about how they might use those materials to engage students in hands-on learning through making.

Ongoing conversations with teachers who showed interest in learning through making was another avenue for attracting volunteers. These conversations resulted in a science teacher providing hands-on science activities during Maker Saturdays and a mathematics teacher designing and starting a small High School Engineering Club. Our collaboration with NuVu Studio resulted in several different studio events or courses where students used making and design thinking to address real-world problems.

As the volunteers increased over time, so did the ownership, and exploration of concrete instances of learning through making at our school. This increased ownership and exploration led to a harvest of insights from successes and failures about what worked and what didn't work for learning through making and tinkering at ASB. These new insights enabled us to focus on incorporating elements that led to improving existing prototypes or creating more successful new prototypes.

Accelerator 5: Accelerate by removing barriers to inquiry
When key players fail to actively support new prototypes, they become barriers to inquiry. This was the case for Making and Tinkering across one division of the school. The existence or absence of the Essential Conditions

for school innovation determine the readiness for innovation. To remove this barrier, the R&D department communicated the missing conditions for successful R&D work, leaving an open invitation to re-engage when there is readiness.

We also re-organized our focus and resources for the Maker Mindset prototyping and began looking for other spaces in the school where interest in learning through making and tinkering and the Essential Conditions were present and growing. Once we identified these spaces in the school, we re-deployed our resources and efforts to support, design, and develop prototypes that would create returns in learning, advance making and tinkering practices, and create small wins that would accelerate a Maker Mindset for teaching and learning. The R&D Operating System is dependent on intrinsically motivated engagement from across the Hierarchy in order to drive inquiries. Without this intrinsic engagement, R&D inquiries don't lead to insights for impactful innovations.

Accelerator 6: Generate and celebrate early impacts

Maker Saturdays, specifically the involvement and engagement of parents in learning through making, were some of the early impacts we celebrated. Maker Saturdays resulted in parents purchasing making materials and setting up maker spaces in their homes. The creation of the TRAI and the GSES prototypes engaging high school students to use making and tinkering to meet real world challenges also grew in popularity, and showed how High School students from around the world might use making and tinkering to create new businesses and solve problems in their world.

Middle School Students collaborating to make Solar Bots during Studio 6

The Studio 6 prototype in the Middle School provided students and teachers with opportunities to teach and learn through making. Student and teacher feedback resulted in expanding that prototype from 2 to 4 days this year. A small successful Maker class in the high school yielded insights and created change capital that enabled R&D to offer three new electives where students will learn primarily using design thinking, programming, and making. High School students increasingly engage in making during their free periods.

Accelerator 7: Keep learning from evidence and experience

As the different short term impacts and making prototypes go through different iterations and spark new impacts and practices, we are starting to understand how to make them better. Making and Tinkering is passing the eye-test at ASB (specifically in two divisions) and in many schools around the world. When we compare the impact of teaching and learning through making today with the impact it was having in the early days of our prototype, we see how it is becoming a significant way that many students at ASB experience learning. However, seeing as believing is not enough to drive successful school R&D. Systematically gathering and analyzing data are key to accelerating a valid successful inquiry.

Gathering data in order to research the impacts of learning through making is a primary focus for accelerating the Maker Mindset prototype. We have created surveys for parents, students, and teachers aimed at understanding the impact of learning through making and tinkering on students. We have developed instruments for assessing learning through making and tinkering in the classroom. These include instruments that students can use to self-report their learning, and instruments that teachers can use to assess the effectiveness of a lesson plan or assess student learning during instances of making. Additionally, we are exploring other domains of assessment that may reveal important impacts of learning through making such as increased motivation for learning and creativity.

An ongoing push to learn from experience with Maker is driving us to inquire and explore the possible impacts of making and tinkering at the intersections of design, fashion, technology, robotics and artificial intelligence, social entrepreneurship and entrepreneurship. New prototyping is revealing new possibilities and new needs for many of our students who are quickly gaining skill and knowledge as they learn at these intersections. Their learning at these intersection is resulting in new knowledge and skills that exceed the knowledge and skills of their teachers.

At this stage other important questions are driving our inquiry. What parts of the Maker Mindset will R&D continue to explore once the prototype is over? What are the resources, programs and structures, and who are the leaders who will sustain learning through making in the future? Continuing to grow prototypes by gathering data is accelerating our inquiry into the Maker Mindset, and resulting in new knowledge and capacity for creating and sustaining prototypes which may become lasting high-impact practices within the Hierarchy Operating System.

CHAPTER 10

Accelerating Studio 6

In the fall of 2013, in partnership with NuVu Studio, the Cambridge based innovation studio, ASB established the Middle School Studio 6 Prototype. Based on the Elementary School Day 9 Prototype, Studio 6 sought to develop the additional facets of learning through a design thinking process, learning through making and tinkering, and cross-curricular learning connected to ASB subject-area standards and benchmarks. Modifications of time, partnership between NuVu Coaches and ASB teachers, and development of Interdisciplinary Learning Studios are key components of this Middle School Prototype.

Accelerator 1: Focus on a high-impact opportunity

The Accelerators – Adapted from John Kotter (2014)

Focus on Studio 6 as a high-impact opportunity developed out of a previous prototype. While key components of the Studio 6 prototype such as cross-curricular learning, project-based learning, design   thinking, and 21st

century skills are driven by global and educational trends, the key driver of Studio 6 was a successful ASB prototype in the Elementary School called Day 9. This prototype was developed by seven elementary educators who were presented with an extra day on the calendar and challenged to answer the question, "If you could create a new day of learning in the Elementary School, what would that look like?" The following were the core elements of design for the prototype day of school:

- Day-long, Project-Based Learning
- High degree of student choice
- Multi-age groupings

Day 9 Students learning about nature in an urban environment

After three iterations of prototyping and data gathering we found that Day 9 was impacting students. The Elementary School Day 9 Prototype resulted in:

- A high degree of student enthusiasm during Day 9 Projects
- A high degree of student engagement during Day 9 Projects
- The significant presence of collaboration during Day 9 Projects
- Positive Learning during Day 9 Projects

- Teachers and teaching assistants reporting significant professional growth and development. (ES Day 9 Report)

These findings and the experience of prototyping the ES Day 9 provided the evidence insights, school context, and created positive momentum for inquiring into how a different day of learning in the Middle School might result in a high-impact opportunity.

Accelerator 2: Attract and maintain an inquiring coalition

Two members of the R&D department and the Middle School Principal formed the Inquiring Coalition for Studio 6. There was a shared interest in how elements of the Day 9 Prototype might be built upon or remixed in order to create a new day of learning in the Middle School. What would that new day look like? How would a new day of learning impact teaching and learning in the Middle School? Once the Inquiring Coalition formed around this opportunity, they began meeting and asking these questions in order to begin envisioning impact and designing a prototype.

Accelerator 3: Envision impact and design a prototype

Starting with the core elements of PBL, student choice, and learning in multi-age groupings, the Inquiring Coalition envisioned students participating in learning studios with these six key elements:
- Project-Based Learning
- Cross-curricular learning
- ASB Standards and Benchmarks
- Making and Tinkering
- Design Thinking
- 21st Century Skills

Once the core elements for the Studio 6 Prototype were mapped out, the Inquiring Coalition took the decision to partner with NuVu Studio in order to co-design 11 interdisciplinary learning studios that would be led by coaches from NuVu and supported by ASB teachers.

Significant strategic consideration went into planning how the new prototype could be created and launched with minimal impact on teachers who were already committed to a busy cycle of planning and teaching. These plans included setting aside times to meet with NuVu Studio, planning logistics, ordering materials, and sharing the prototype with the Middle School Faculty Leadership Team (MSLT) in order to solicit feedback and ideas on the role of ASB teachers during the prototype.

Studio 6 Students learning how to use their cameras for their documentary studio

Accelerator 4: Attract volunteer inquirers

Even though a concrete vision and a prototype had been formed, the decision to carefully consider the existing workload of teachers resulted in a strategic choice by the Inquiring Coalition to delay inviting volunteer inquirers (which would be the typical next step for prototyping new teaching practices in a school). This choice had several impacts.

- The Inquiring coalition was able to create and launch the prototype without overloading faculty and killing the new prototype.
- Using NuVu Coaches to design and lead real-world learning studios provided as a new model for teaching and learning in our school.
- Teachers were freed up to participate, observe, consider, and reflect on the real-world studio model for teaching and learning.

Middle School Students engaged in the Wearable Tech Studio

Deciding not to invite volunteer inquirers led to a successful launch of the prototype and increased understanding and readiness for teaching and learning through real-world interdisciplinary learning studios. However, the absence of volunteer inquirers emerged as a barrier to accelerating Studio 6.

Accelerator 5: Accelerate by removing barriers to inquiry

Through conversations with teachers and data collected during the second iteration of Studio 6, the Inquiring Coalition identified the absence of volunteers as a significant barrier to inquiry into Studio 6. Ensuring the successful launch and building readiness were prerequisites to engaging faculty as volunteer inquirers. Now, however, there is a need to open up the prototype and invite volunteers to begin participating as owners, designing, teaching, and making important adjustments that improve and grow the Studio 6 prototype and provide energy and engagement that will accelerate the inquiry.

To address and remove this barrier, the Inquiring Coalition will invite and support teachers who have experienced previous Studios to take lead roles by designing, coaching, and developing a few Studios for the next iteration of the prototype in Spring 2016.

CHAPTER 11

Accelerating Learning Analytics

While collecting data is nothing new for educational organizations, much of the data that is collected exists in a variety of formats, systems, and departments. This disconnected data makes it difficult to use it in ways that lead to increased understanding for teaching and learning. New tools for measuring, collecting, analyzing and reporting data are dramatically changing how schools can use data to optimize learning. As technology rapidly accelerates, Learning Analytics and Data Visualization may lead to high-impact opportunities for teaching and learning success.

Accelerating 1: Focus on a high-impact opportunity

The Accelerators – Adapted from John Kotter (2014)

R&D of Learning Analytics is driven by global trends. In their 2013 Horizon Report on K-12 Education, the New Media Consortium identifies Learning Analytics as a trend that will enter the mainstream of adoption in schools by 2016. The Institute For The Future, in their report, *The Information Generation Transforming the Future,* states the following:

"The world is different and will never be the same again. The four mega-trends of big data, always-connected mobile devices, social networking, and cloud computing are reshaping industries, redefining experiences and fortifying sustainable businesses" (IFTF, 2015). These trends don't exist somewhere in a distant future; they are already becoming integrated into our everyday lives. From the devices our students use, carry and wear, to the courses they take, and how they socially connect, our students are living and learning differently.

Learning Analytics Prototype at ASB is also an example of how emerging trends can become sudden opportunities for schools in an accelerating change environment. What started as an exploration of a promising future trend for schools in the spring of 2014, has quickly become an important practice for our present, requiring fast, focused R&D of practices, approaches, and new tools for using data visualization and learning analytics in schools. The potential for Data Visualizations and Learning Analytics to help us understand and optimize learning for each of our learners in their rapidly changing learning contexts is the clear primary driver of our decisions and actions for accelerating Learning Analytics at ASB.

Accelerator 2: Attract and maintain an inquiring coalition
This prototype started when the R&D department met with a data scientist and worked on a project to visualize data from a survey of high school students about their experiences taking online courses at ASB. This visualization brought all of the data from the survey together on a single page and made it possible to explore relationships between the data as well as to inquire into the data by interacting with the visualization. From there, the R&D department created a series of data visualizations and quickly evolved as the Inquiring Coalition for the Learning Analytics prototype. Exploring learning analytics with a talented data scientist jump-started the awareness, curiosity, and a sense of urgency for accelerating an inquiry into the opportunity that learning analytics have for teaching and learning at ASB.

Accelerator 3: Envision impact and design a prototype
With the ability to create a wide array of tools to visualize data, the R&D department began envisioning how to best use Learning Analytics to transform teaching and learning. They started by putting together an initial

list of aims for learning analytics at ASB. They envisioned that Learning Analytics at ASB should:

- Catalyze conversations about student learning
- Enable learners to reflect on their data.
- Support individual student learning
- Enable a holistic view of student learning over time
- Enable teachers to plan instruction for groups and individuals
- Improve and inform the development of learning opportunities
- Inform institutional decision making

Once the vision began taking shape, R&D decided to create a kind of "baseball card" (now known as Student Data Profiles) that could enable an observer to see a wide array of student data visually represented on a single page. This triggered strategic decisions about which data would be most useful to visualize first. It resulted in the creation of timelines for designing these visualizations as well as plans for engaging volunteers to beta test the Student Data Profiles.

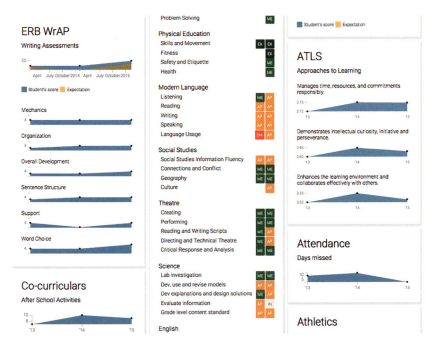

Snapshot of a Student Data Profile

Accelerator 4: Attract volunteer inquirers

After developing a suite of prototype data visualizations, R&D invited division principals and individuals who worked intensively with specific data to begin prototyping, forming a team of volunteers. We also introduced the following Data WOCQ protocol to support inquiring educators to use the data to develop new connections, questions, and insights, before moving into creating solutions.

Data WOCQ - A quick guide for walking through data

- **W**onderings - What do you find yourself wondering about as you look through the data? Wonder, discuss, uncover but don't jump to conclusions.
- **O**bservations - Look for patterns. What are you seeing? What are the outliers? What are the surprises?
- **C**onnections - Start to connect the data with your background experiences with a student, a class, a grade level, a school, a curriculum, other variables and other data.
- **Q**uestions - What are the questions you find you need to think about, talk about, or act upon?

Individuals who work intensively with data like MAP or literacy were the first volunteers to provide specific feedback that led to changes. These encouraged more use and engagement with the data. For example, a literacy coach suggested changes to the visualization of Fountas and Pinnell reading assessment data. This immediately resulted in a data visualization she could use to plan instruction with teachers.

On the division level, one division uses the Student Data Profiles in whole-faculty meetings where they look at data to discuss and make plans to support individual students. These are the heaviest users of the student data profiles. Their ideas and feedback have led to the greatest changes of the data visualizations, and have increased use and exploration of other contexts for using the profiles.

Another division created a committee to envision how the student data profiles might be used in the classroom or as a live transcript that could follow students to other schools. However the division didn't employ the student data profiles for these specific purposes and contexts, or communicate clearly that faculty could use them. Limiting the engagement of volunteer users had the effect of limiting the inquiry, awareness, and development of the student data profiles for that division.

Another division shared the student data profiles with other educators but did not establish purposes or contexts for using them. Without a focus or a vision for use, engagement by volunteers in this division is low and has not led to changes in the student data profiles or how they can be used.

Ownership, clear purposes, and intentionally providing feedback has resulted in volunteers, as well as increased usefulness and usage among educators at ASB. Where these factors aren't present, there are fewer voluntary inquirers using the learning analytics tools, and making changes to develop and improve the usefulness and usage of the tools that have been created. Going forward the work of Accelerator 4 is not complete. Accelerating the prototype will required more volunteer inquirers. However, at the end of a year of prototyping Learning Analytics, we are seeing clear advantages over previous systems for using student data to support teaching and learning. The student profiles have become increasingly visible throughout the school; approximately one-third of the school has been actively inquiring, using, and improving the profiles to meet their needs for supporting student learning. These insights will inform how R&D will manage the prototype to increase the volunteer inquirers. If R&D is not able to attract and increase the volunteers going forward, a lack of volunteers may pose barriers that threaten the inquiry into Learning Analytics.

CHAPTER 12

Accelerating Social Entrepreneurships

Accelerator 1: Focus on a high-impact opportunity

Focus on Social Entrepreneurship as a high-impact opportunity for our school lies at the intersection of our school's mission and core values, and the importance of social entrepreneurship in our country. According to the Overseas Indian Facilitation Centre (OIFC), India has the largest number of social enterprises in the world (OIFC, 2014). Other trends are causing us to challenge our own assumptions about what young people want and need for their lives. The Stanford Social Innovation Review notes the following:

The Accelerators – Adapted from John Kotter (2014)

Half the people living in the world today are under the age of 30. The hundreds of millions of young people born in the digital age are more informed and connected than ever before. They've grown up in an era of widespread democracy, with expectations of freedom and equality. They are aware and distressed by the environmental, economic, and political state of the world. Change is very much on their minds: The world we have is not the one that they want. The interest of young people in change making is manifest in the surge in social entrepreneurship programs on college campuses and in young people taking to the street en masse for a slew of causes: against economic disparity in the Occupy Movement in the United States, for political representation in the Arab

Spring, against corruption via the Lokpal Bill in India, and for affordable education in the Chilean Student Movement. These movements represent the readiness of young people to organize and vocalize their concerns. (SSIR, 2014)

In a survey on workforce readiness by the Center for Creative Leadership, Van Velsor & Wright report that executives viewed young workers as not getting the experiences they needed to prepare them for the workforce. They cited a lack of self-motivation, communication skills, learning agility, self-awareness and adaptability as common traits of their younger colleagues (Van Velsor & Wright, 2012).

These trends pointed to social entrepreneurship as a business model that could:
- provide young people with the global impact they are seeking
- help young people gain workforce skills they lack through authentic learning experience.

Accelerator 2: Attract and maintain an inquiring coalition
In the fall of 2013, a small cadre of students in the High School began engaging with each other and posting and commenting on topics ranging from poverty, gender issues, education inequity, to freedom of expression through a website called Student News Action. Their activity triggered conversations between a classroom teacher and the R&D Department. These conversations resulted in the teacher and the R&D department forming the Inquiring Coalition for social entrepreneurship. The Inquiring Coalition envisioned how these increasingly connected students might move past dialog, and make an impact on these global issues. These visioning conversations eventually led the Inquiring Coalition to wonder how social entrepreneurship might meet students' needs to learn and have a global impact.

Accelerator 3: Envision impact and design a prototype
The Inquiring Coalition began by envisioning a way that engaged students from ASB might be able to take action to solve the problems they were increasingly passionate about. The result was creating a prototype Global Social Entrepreneurship Summit (GSES) where students would:

- Organize and lead the conference.
- Explore and study Social Entrepreneurship.
- Learn from Social Entrepreneurs in the workforce.
- Use Design Thinking to develop empathy and acquire knowledge in order to design a social business to meet human needs.
- Create and pitch a business plan.

After envisioning the impact for students and deciding on the key elements for the Summit, the Inquiring Coalition created a plan and a timeline for engaging volunteers to research, plan, coordinate and lead the prototype summit.

Accelerator 4: Attract voluntary inquirers

The call for volunteers went out to students in the High School and resulted in eight students volunteering to lead and participate in the Summit. In the months before the Summit, these students met for several Saturdays and after school, planning sessions where they studied and explored Social Entrepreneurship, visited social enterprises, read about social enterprises, and planned their roles and responsibilities for leading the Summit. In February 2014, at the GSES, the eight volunteer inquirers led 35 students to create four social enterprises designed to meet important human needs of food waste, education, lack of awareness in Indian politics, and violence against women. The GSES is now planning for a third iteration and consideration is being given to how promising social enterprises developed during the third Summit might be supported, developed, and established as sustainable social businesses.

In January 2015 additional volunteers joined an R&D Staff Task Force where they are exploring, studying, researching and proposing prototypes that might expand opportunities and engage more volunteers in accelerating the inquiry into how Social Entrepreneurship may impact teaching and learning.

CHAPTER 13

Making New Choices

Innovative schools create new choices that lead to new opportunities and new decisions. Tim Brown, the CEO of IDEO captures this in the following...

> "If you are just looking at the same set of choices as everybody else is looking at, you're likely to get to the same innovations that they are. But if however, you can create new choices, choices that nobody else is looking at, that nobody else has seen, there's a pretty strong chance that you can get to an innovation that nobody else has gotten to." (Brown, 2009)

This chapter has five real world stories that are examples of newly created choices that are leading to new opportunities and new decisions at ASB - decisions that wouldn't have been available to us without a systematic approach to innovation. As you read these stories, think about your context and how this applies to you - the culture and the essential conditions, the impetus for change, the engagement of the stakeholders, and the accelerators that made change happen.

Creating the future of a school doesn't happen overnight. It is a day to day process of exploring, studying, prototyping, researching, and scaling that enables a school to sustainably innovate and create new choices.

In the previous chapters we've shared the why, the how, the when, and the who of R&D, all in ASB's context. Now it's time for you to apply this to your context and lead change. It is the contexts of your school, your community, and your educators that will provide the insights, understandings, and learning to enable you to invent the future of your school.

Example 1

New Media in Art: Where Does the Art Happen?

(This section is written by Karen Fish & Karishma Galani and published in *Future Forwards*, Volume 3)

New Media in Art

Technology is part of young people's DNA. Using new media in the creation of an artwork is not something new. Look what John Goffe Rand's invention of the paint tube in 1841 did to painting! What's new is the rapid growth in cheap accessible technology available to be co-opted for creative purposes.

Young people are not afraid of technology. In fact they are often more afraid of traditional art media. Ask them to draw and they will quiver with fear. Ask them to use their computer to edit an image and there is no hesitation. Using new media allows art students to take that comfort level with technology and link it with their creative and critical thinking to create new and sometimes unexpected art.

Any contemporary gallery or museum that one visits today is full of examples of work that involves the use of technology. At first I wondered "Wow. How did they do that?" But now what I'm coming to realize is that the technology employed is often not that complicated. Rather what makes it art is the 'idea' that drives the artwork and is communicated to the audience.

The Idea is the Most Important Thing

I saw a recent exhibition in Paris at the Centre Pompidou where clothing was suspended from the ceiling. Using motors and a little programming the clothing danced. It was lyrical and quite beautiful. My students loved it and we all stood mesmerized. Then one of them said, "We could make that." Another said, "Yeah we could, but we didn't think of it..." And they were right. It is the idea, not the technology; that is where the art lies. They did not stand in front of a Leonardo da Vinci in the Louvre and say I can do that! So what this means to me is that the revolution in art is that using new media makes the idea the most important thing. It is all about the thinking. For centuries art has been about the development of exquisite and highly developed skills. Now it is becoming more and more about the concept.

Students' Experience
In mid-September, the ASB welcomed forty art students from all over Asia to take part in the SAISA Arts Festival held in Mumbai. This three day event offered students with three tracks: sculpting, painting, and new media. Students chose one track to be immersed in for the three days of the festival. Members of the R&D department worked with us to run the new media in art track. The theme was Contra/plexity: The Contrasts and Complexity of this Megacity, Mumbai.

What Does New Media in Art Look Like?
During the planning stages, we decided that the following tools would be a good place for students to start exploring this.

Electronics
Electronics in art is all about simple machines and how to incorporate motors, batteries, or LEDs into the piece to support the students' message. Similar to

The student attaching a motor to her art piece

The student's end-product using a motor

the flying curtains example, a few students used a motor to symbolize the rotation of time. One student attached a motor to a circular piece of cardstock board and placed doors made with cardboard that represented the range of socio-economic disparities seen in Mumbai. The rotation of the motor represented two sides of the same coin of Mumbai.

3D Modeling and Printing

3D printing in art is more about modeling your piece through a software such as Blender or Google Sketchup and then setting it up to print through a 3D printer. The process of 3D modeling can be challenging and requires persistence. However, watching the model print is rewarding! The art happens in the modeling, and students are only just being exposed to that concept. About half the group explore 3D modelling. One of them modeled her final art piece and printed it on the 3D printer.

A student talking about her 3D model with her 3D printed car

Laser Cutting

A machine that uses a laser beam to cut through various materials with precision, the laser cutter opened up endless possibilities for the students. Similar to 3D printing, the laser cutting part wasn't tricky, as much as figuring out what you wanted laser cut, and if the idea was going to be enhanced by this specific tool. One student etched and laser cut parts of photographs she had taken the first day during the field trips around Mumbai. Her piece was primarily on women in India and the challenges they face in their day-to-day experiences.

A student's end product

Aside from these main elements, students also had access to Arduino programming boards, stencil cutters, 3D pens, and all other art supplies like paints, glue, and cardboard.

The important aspect of exploring new media is the excitement students have while using it. Take 3D printing for example; about half the students started off exploring it. However, they quickly realized that downloading a pattern and printing it is not art. It is not even a little bit creative. Technology is taking us to a place where it is not the skills that make the art, it is the message you want to convey. That's where the Idea begins: why would it respond that way, what does it mean, why is that happening? These questions are where the art happens.

Example 2

Designing a Balanced School Calendar

(This section is written by Paul Kasky & Shabbi Luthra and published in *Future Forwards,* Volume 1)

Time is one of our most precious and limited resources. An evaluation of the use of this resource is essential for schools to truly personalize student learning. For centuries, schools around the world have followed agrarian school calendars. The purpose behind these calendars - to allow children to help their families during planting or harvest times - is now moot; no one disagrees with its "mootness". This has opened the conversation anew regarding what type of school calendar would best support student learning. This includes evaluating the timing and duration of academic terms, vacations, possible intersession periods, and teacher contracts.

In spring 2012, ASB's R&D Team studied school year calendars. The study process included the following:

- Research on the impact of long summer vacations (defined as any vacation beyond six weeks in length) on student learning loss.
- Research on the effects of various alternative school year schedules on student learning in schools where alternative calendars have been employed.
- Study of various school year calendars, including single-track and multi-track models.
- Survey to gather data on the travel habits and vacation preferences of our parent community, including the types of academic enrichment and remediation opportunities they sought for their children.
- Survey to gather data on our teachers' perceptions of the need for alternative calendar consideration, including their own travel

and vacation preferences, academic needs of students, and contract and professional development opportunities.

Findings

Below are some of the findings of our study and research.

- Based on current and recent studies, students experience the equivalent of 2.6 months of grade-level equivalency loss in math. While students from middle class families actually experience a slight gain in overall reading performance over a traditional summer break, reading comprehension decreases after summer vacation (National Center for Summer Learning, Johns Hopkins University, 2009; Reading Is Fundamental, 2009).
- According to the 2012 Carson-Dellosa Summer Learning Study, 85% of teachers spend two-plus weeks at the beginning of the school year re-teaching critical skills forgotten from the previous year, and 41% report spending a month or more (Carson-Dellosa, 2012).
- According to H. Cooper, "Meta-analysis indicated that summer learning loss equaled at least one month of instruction as measured by grade level equivalents on standardized test scores - on average, children's tests scores were at least one month lower when they returned to school in fall than scores were when students left in spring" (Cooper, 2003).
- Children whose primary language is not English suffer the greatest summer learning loss. "Changing the school calendar could make a great difference in language skill development for these students" (Ballinger, 1995). Our school has a significant population of learners whose home language is not English.
- A balanced school year schedule can include intersessions or non-vacation breaks during the school year. During these intersessions, a school can offer a variety of enrichment and remediation programs as well as test-prep courses for SAT, ACT, and IB Test preparation. In addition, the school can utilize community partnerships that allow students, particularly high school students, to engage in internships and other experiential learning opportunities (Ballinger & Kneese, 2006; 70-72). All of

- this supports and enhances our school's goal of personalizing student learning.
- The National Association for Year-Round Education (NAYRE), a think tank that studies and researches school year calendars, recommends that vacation periods are no longer than six weeks. However, they will accept up to eight weeks for inclusion in its national directory of year-round schools (Ballinger & Kneese, 2006; 51).
- Intersession programs are an effective way to limit summer learning loss. These summer programs should conclude very near the beginning of the following school year to most effectively limit and make up for any summer learning loss that occurs (National Summer Learning Association, 2009).
- In schools already implementing various alternative school year schedules, evidence about student improvement is ambiguous because of limited data, small sample sizes and even conflicting data. Though gains are large for lower-performing students, they are less clear for others. However, students, parents, and teachers who are stakeholders in schools with these schedules are "overwhelmingly positive about the experience" (Cooper, 2003).
- In spite of the findings in the statement above, it is important to note that according to Shields and Oberg, "balanced calendars do often provide the conditions under which more children can learn to higher levels of achievement than in traditional-calendar schools." Moreover, no studies have ever provided evidence that a balanced school calendar has a detrimental impact on student learning, "indeed, the most critical findings have been 'no impact'" (Shields & Oberg, 2009, p. 40).
- According to the task force's ASB parent survey, nearly all families (94%) spend the majority of their current ten-week summer vacation outside of Mumbai. A majority (61%) of parents, however, would prefer a shorter summer vacation of six to eight weeks.
- 68% of parent respondents indicated that they would consider enrolling a child in an ASB summer program (intersession) if it

suited the child's needs. The majority of those respondents (52%) communicated that they would prefer a two-week intersession period for their child, while 35% would prefer a longer, four-week intersession.

- According to the task force's ASB teacher survey, 91% of teachers acknowledge a summer learning slide for students given our current ten-week summer vacation.
- 93% of teacher respondents spend at least half of their summer vacation time outside of India traveling or in their home countries.
- 77% of teacher respondents indicated that a summer vacation between six and eight weeks in length would be "ideal" for students.
- While a strong majority of teacher respondents (68%) indicated that the current one-week fall break is "just right", 43% of respondents shared that the one-week spring break is "too short".
- 33% of teachers respondents indicated that lengthening the winter vacation to four or five weeks would be "ideal", though a majority feel that it is "just right" at three weeks.
- When considering student needs, 47% of teachers demonstrated satisfaction with the current (approximately) 180 days of student contact. However 46% indicated a preference for an increase of between 200 and 220 days of student contact. In the survey, the option to increase student contact days was accompanied by the statement that those 200 days "could include summer school".
- 71% of teacher respondents showed a preference for an increase in the number of *teacher choice* professional development days as a component of their contracts. 53% prefer a model that includes ten days of teacher choice PD, while another 18% prefer a 15-20 day model.
- When given several alternatives, only 20% of teachers indicated a preference for the current 5/8 teaching, 3/8 planning teacher day model. The remaining 80% would prefer to make coaching and/or mentoring a contracted part of their day, and 44% would

elect to reduce their teaching load from 5/8 to either 4/8 or 3/8 in order to do that.

- "Researchers have pointed out that teachers go through certain developmental stages as they progress in their careers, each of which triggers specific needs and crises that they must address." The standardized nature of traditional professional development programs assumes that all teachers should perform at the same level, regardless of their particular experience and needs. It is important that teachers have personal choice in professional development to meet their individual growth needs (Diaz-Maggioli, 2004).

Recommendations

Based on the findings above, the R&D Team made the following recommendations in its report.

- *Implementation of a new, more balanced school year calendar -* It is clear that all students would benefit from a shortened summer vacation that lasts no longer than six weeks. After reviewing dozens of single-track and multi-track calendar models, accounting for the various expectations and preferences of teachers and parents through surveys, and recognizing the home-visit needs of an expat population of families and teachers, the following changes to the current calendar were recommended for consideration.
  - o Reducing the summer vacation from ten weeks to six weeks.
  - o Redistribution of the four vacation weeks that have been removed from the summer vacation as follows:
    - The addition of two weeks of vacation to winter break, creating a five-week vacation.
    - The addition of one week of vacation to the fall term, creating two weeks of fall vacation.
    - The addition of one week of vacation to the spring term, creating two weeks of spring vacation.

- *Creation of a summer intersession* - Regardless of any other changes to the overall ASB calendar, a summer intersession period will ensure that students who are in need of academic remediation or enrichment have the opportunity to mitigate the impact of a substantial summer vacation. A summer intersession should provide a variety of academic remediation and enrichment courses in multiple disciplines in order to ensure personalized growth and learning for each student. Additionally, ASB should offer two separate two-week intersessions during the summer to provide flexibility to students who travel with their families during the vacation. The last intersession should end within two weeks of the start of the next school year.
- *Creation of a winter Intersession* - A winter intersession would provide an additional opportunity for personalized and enhanced student growth and would limit any learning loss that results from a lengthened winter vacation.
- *Flexibility in teacher contracts for Professional Development* - Based on research and teacher survey preference indications, the task force recommends that teacher contracts include increased time and flexibility in teacher choice professional development. A model that permits teachers approximately ten days for a combination of teacher choice PD attendance, reflection and implementation outside of the classroom is recommended. Continuity in the classes of teachers attending increased professional development would be supported by the continued use of avatar and novice teacher positions, student teachers and interns. Additionally, the task force recommends consideration of increased PD funding for teachers to further support this recommendation. The R&D task force is currently investigating and designing a model for increased personalization of teacher choice professional development.
- *Flexibility in teacher contracts for alternative school roles* - Based on teacher strengths and interests, the task force recommends further research and consideration of increased flexibility in the use of teachers' contracted time. ASB currently follows a common model in which 5/8 of teachers' time is spent teaching

while 3/8 is for planning and meetings. As student needs and teacher strengths and preferences change, ASB can consider ways in which it can adjust teacher roles to best meet the various needs of students and utilize teacher strengths.

- *Parent Education* - According to the parent survey results, the vast majority of parents preferred a summer vacation of eight to ten weeks. This preference does not agree with the research that clearly demonstrates that learning loss occurs in vacations of that length. Educating the parent community about the findings and the benefits of a more balanced schedule is essential.

The Task Force's research leads us to conclude that our 20th century school calendars need to be deconstructed and then super-structed on principles that better serve student learning. Though there are inevitably challenges whenever systems are disrupted, there is clearly an urgency for schools to engage in conversations about balanced school calendars that support student learning.

Example 3

SOCIAL ENTREPRENEURS:
Innovators with an Unreasonable Vision

(This section is written by Karishma Galani and published in *Future Forwards*, Volume 1)

A social entrepreneur looks at the world's biggest problems as a window of opportunity. They are motivated and passionate about disrupting the system and designing solutions for the world's harshest, and often too big to fix, social problems. One of the examples that resonates with me is William Foote, founder of Root Capital, a nonprofit social investment fund. Its clients are groups of farmers who lack access to capital that could help sustain their business and help them compete effectively in today's economy. These businesses are too large for microfinance but risky for banks to invest in. Foote believes in filling this gap and formed Root Capital, a bank for the missing middle.

An Unreasonable Vision

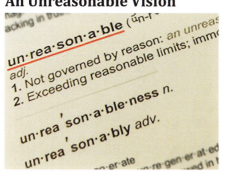

Foote isn't the only one who came up with an innovative and disruptive solution to a seemingly impossible social issue. Muhammad Yunus, Dr. V, and Paul Farmer have also dedicated their lives to making their dreams, and those of millions of others, come to life. They all had one thing in common: their unreasonable vision. Whether it was to eradicate poverty through access to working capital in Bangladesh, cure avoidable blindness in India for little to no cost, or even provide world class healthcare for villagers in Haiti, they dreamt big. These are dreams that many said were impossible to achieve, and yet today, we have Grameen Bank, Aravind Eye Care, and Partners in Health standing strong (and growing) to address these challenges. They are all social innovators who are passionate, engaged, and always thinking of innovative ways to bring large scale change.

Grameen Bank   Arvind Eye

Who Can Be A Social Entrepreneur?

Anyone with ambition, persistence, and the motivation to help improve current social challenges can be a social entrepreneur. Following a human centered approach, social entrepreneurs are hungry and passionate to see their communities transform regardless of their age, profession, and experience.

A 16 year-old From California

Hayley Hoverter, 16 years old, created soluble, paperless organic sugar packets because she realized that sugar packets contribute to the 40% of paper waste found in landfills. She sells these products all over California now. Students can learn about marketing, communicating, making a pitch, and creating a powerful positive impact through  something that they feel strongly connected with. But the most important skill they learn through this process is to address complex and "too big to fix" social issues through smaller, manageable action steps. These skills are essential, not just for personal growth, but for the transformation of our society. This is what President Barack Obama had to say about Haley:

"What impresses me is not just how smart you are, but the fact that you recognize you've got a responsibility to use your talents in service of something bigger than yourselves. For some, that means developing new products that will change the way we live. Hayley Hoverter invented a new type of sugar packet that dissolves in hot water. It's flavorless, it's colorless, and could potentially save up to 2 million pounds of trash each year — and that's just at Starbucks."

Our Students

Like Haley, all students can create a powerful social impact too. All they need are the right tools and access to likeminded individuals who believe passionately about their own unreasonable visions. In February 2014, ASB is hosting the first **Global Social Entrepreneurship Summit** – www.asbunplugged.org/gses.htm where students from schools around the world will have the opportunity to gather in Mumbai and address social challenges they feel passionate about.

GSES

Using a design thinking process, students will collaborate to learn about and create innovative solutions to challenging social problems. These social challenges will be ones that students identify from their home countries. During the Summit, they will interact with and learn from social entrepreneurs in India. They will learn about the importance of sustainability, the issues of scalability, and how technology can be a game changer in reaching their goals. By the end of the Summit, students will have designed a business and marketing plan to prototype their disruptive solution. They will return to their school, community or city with their solution and a plan to implement. Students would have learned to apply the design processes to other social challenges they encounter. We hope they will see opportunities even in the most complex social challenges and become social innovators.

Example 4

Shifting Tides: "Day 9", a New Day of Learning

(This section is written by Shannon Gallagher & Scot Hoffman and published in *Future Forwards*, Volume 1)

A perfect storm: an expression that describes an event where a rare combination of circumstance will aggravate [or disrupt] a situation drastically. The term is also used to describe an actual phenomenon that happens to occur in such a confluence, resulting in an event of unusual magnitude (Wikipedia).

Without realizing it, the elementary school at the American School of Bombay, had all the elements of a perfect storm brewing. Within the past year and a half, one task force had focused on the implications of Multi-Age Classrooms, another on Project-Based Learning, the elementary school had shifted to a campus with collaborative learning spaces, and there was an unmarked day on the calendar. The tide was turning.

In his book, *Creative Intelligence: Harnessing the Power to Create, Connect, and Inspire*, author Bruce Nussbaum introduces a concept he calls VUCA. It stands for "Volatile, Uncertain, Complex, and Ambiguous". He cites these landscapes of conditions as challenging, but also as opportunities to think, collaborate, and do things differently. This was precisely the situation in February 2013 as a team of teachers from the elementary school sat down to create a "new school day".

After much brainstorming, discussion, confusion, and moments of clarity the team began to shape the vision for this new day. It would be a day that facilitated student and teacher choice and interest; a day that required students to grapple with a driving question; a day for teachers to get their feet wet with some of the key elements of project-based learning; a day where students of different age levels and grades were able to come together to form Multi-Age groupings; a day completely unlike anything that had happened in the elementary school before.

Thus, the title for the day, "Day 9," seemed fitting. The school calendar at ASB, has been based on a six day rotation, an eight day rotation, and even a "color day" rotation, but there had never been a ninth day... until now.

In his book, Nussbaum also mentions "magic circles". He describes these as small groups of people who trust each other to play at experimenting and discovering new things. Our team of eight, continued to come together to refine, plan, and develop Day 9. Through a willingness to fail, take risks, and make mistakes, the expected outcomes and goals began to rise to the surface. Our "magic circle" decided the goals of Day 9 would be:

- To provide students and teachers with an experience in a day-long project-based inquiry.
- To provide a high degree of choice for students and teachers.
- To provide students and teachers with an experience of multi-age learning teams.

Yet this is not an easy feat for a single day on the school-year calendar. Creating a project-based learning experience can take hours, even weeks to plan - especially for someone who is unfamiliar with the elements that define and shape these inquiry-based projects. Also, very few teachers in the elementary school had ever had an experience working with multi-age groups of learners. Over the next few weeks, we would be asking teachers to:

- Decide upon an area of interest or passion.
- Develop and refine a driving question, open enough to allow for student choice and inquiry - but focused enough to ensure understanding and connection.
- Adapt their project to a Multi-Age group of learners, either grades K to 2 or grades 3 to 5.
- Think about a way for students to share, by the end of their day together, an aspect of their Day 9 experience with the school-wide community.
- Throw out their traditional schedule and to create a plan for one day as an open-ended, inquiry-based project.

Many challenges presented themselves. From supporting teachers' understanding of project-based learning, to logistical challenges of determining how to schedule snack and recess for our newly formed Multi-Age learning teams. Determining how to provide student choice while maintaining a balanced multi-age group, was another unique hurdle that caused the team of eight to head back to the drawing board.

But in time, schedules were created, teachers were supported (both in school-wide faculty meetings and in one-on-one sessions, when requested), and a protocol was created in which each grade level class was given the opportunity to choose from a selection of the project options available at their grade level (to ensure balanced ages for each project). The storm was moving in.

As Day 9 approached, feelings of uncertainty, excitement, anxiety, and curiosity were palpable. Fifth grade teachers wondered aloud if their plans for a group of kindergartens through second graders would hold up. Others wondered about the materials, space, and resources their students might need as the day progressed - because a project truly designed with student-led inquiry at the foreground, necessitates a level of uncertainty. And still others were curious about the flow of the day, because it is not often students have the opportunity to focus on one project for the entire course of the day.

On April 5th 2013, the time for planning was over. The perfect storm was upon the elementary school. Over fifty teachers and teaching assistants had designed, created, and refined their projects. They had the list of students spanning three grade levels who had voiced their interest in their particular project. Resources and learning spaces had been arranged as best as possible to meet the requirements of each project (as much of the needs that could be planned for in advance, anyway). And it was time for the students to arrive.

So what did Day 9 actually look like?
Starting at 8:15 am, grades K to 5 students gathered and moved from their homeroom floors to the floors and learning spaces where their projects would take place. After a brief welcome on their new floors, Multi-Age cohorts of 6 to 12 students went with their instructors to their new learning spaces. Students worked on their projects for three sessions, for about 3.5

Two kindergarten students creating a story using stop-action animation

hours in total. Students also shared lunches and recesses with students, teachers, and teacher assistants they don't typically spend time with, or maybe even know beyond a passing hello.

At 1:45 pm, 364 students exhibited, performed, demonstrated or otherwise shared with peers, the fruits of the 31 different learning projects such as: *Math and Art, Designs with People in Mind, Writing Nonfiction, Reading Fluency through Theater, Music Movement & Maps, Rocket Science, Nature in an Urban Environment, Expressing Yourself Through Poetry, and Math Games for Higher Level Thinking, Reasoning, & Strategies.*

A student building a structure he designed

At 2:20 pm, students returned to their home floors and their home rooms where they buzzed about their day, shared their artifacts, and compared their project experiences.

When the team of eight got back together, we reflected on how we had imagined, designed, and executed this new day, and wondered if we had achieved the results we planned and worked for. Through the lens of teacher feedback, we began to see how each of our aims had resulted in tangible results. The following is a portion of this feedback:

Teachers sharing about their experience with a day-long inquiry project reflected:

- "Kids loved that they were able to concentrate on researching and learning just one topic for the entire day".

- "One student commented that a regular school day was more tiring and I think I felt the same".
- "A 3rd grader who, at the beginning said that there was no nature in India, changed his mind by the end of the day".

Grade 3-5 students making books featuring real children fighting for justice in the world

- "...the best thing was that at the end of the day we sat around in a circle and went round the circle asking for thoughts about the day. Every single student was really enthusiastic about what they had learned and what they had created".

Teacher reflections around student choice:
- "They [students] could go as deep as they wanted in each of their choices".
- "Choosing what I wanted to teach and having students choose my topic set the stage for enjoyment and success".

K-2 students creating art using mathematical shapes and patterns

- "I felt like all of my students arrived at the start of the day excited about something new and excited about the project because they were able to choose it".

Teacher reflections around teaching Multi-Age groups:
- *"Working in Multi-Age groups was fun. Watching the exchange of ideas, involvement in the project and the mentoring was inspiring".*

- "My observation was that all the older children were willing to help the younger ones. The children worked so well that the activity became fun to do".
- "Despite our nervousness about [working with] the little ones, once we met our group it was easier to figure out tweaks to make it age appropriate for the group".
- "I really liked working with a multi-age group. I loved the way that students helped each other".

Two Grade 5 students testing their new cooking skills

Feedback from students was also gathered in the form of randomly selected focus groups from each grade level. Each of these groups were asked to give their feedback and share any other thoughts based on their experience with Day 9. Here is the transcript from a sample of three, fourth grade students:

Teacher: So, I guess I just wanted to find out what was day 9 like for you?
Student 1: Fun.
Student 2: Incredible.
Student 3: Epic... Yeah, epic.
Student 1: I learned a lot- and it was hands-on, which was really fun.
Student 2: Uh huh.
Student 3: Rocket science was epic. I think we should have more day nines.
Student 1: Yep. And maybe we could do different subjects each year.
Student 3: Yeah.
Student 2: And also it was kinda fun, and the mixing with different classes was great to get to know different people and everything.
Student 3: We got to mix with the fifth graders sometimes the first and second graders, third graders as well.
Teacher: What was that like?

Student 2: We got to see what it was like working with different grade levels.

Student 1: They're so much alike to us anyway, so they're not so different to us. It's interesting to be all in one class.

Teacher: If you could change something for day 9 what would you change?

Student 1: Maybe each class would get to pick from a larger amount of subject and maybe more information about the subjects.

Student 2: Yeah, again maybe larger amount subjects, because I only liked two of the subjects out of the five subjects in my class.

Student 3: I would change nothing because I really liked everything. The teachers, friends, stuff like that.

Student 2: Yeah, it's really cool how the teachers were really good at their topic because it's what they picked.

Student 1: Yeah, I loved how the teachers were really in it. They were experts, and it was funny it wasn't just....

Student 2: Learning, learning, learning.

Student 1: Yeah...

Teacher: It was just a different day, right?

All students: Yeah, really different.

Teacher: Any last thoughts or words on day 9?

Student 2: I liked how we got to go around and see what other people did. That was fun.

Student 1: Yeah, we should definitely do this again.

Student 3: Yeah... Yeah. Definitely.

Day 9 2.0

As a result of the data and feedback on our first prototype, two Day 9 learning days were scheduled for the 2013-2014 school year. Planning began in September and focused on adjusting the Day 9 prototype in order to:

- Strengthen professional development and deepen

K-2 students presenting their Reader's Theater skit

faculty understanding of Project-Based Learning.

- Increase student choice options for Day 9 projects.
- Further broaden student project choices.
- Maximize opportunities for sharing Day 9 outcomes across the school.
- Include students in designing and developing Day 9 at ASB.

The November 1st Day 9 Prototype was another successful learning day. It continued to meet the goals it was designed for. Professional development helped the projects to be increasingly focused by engaging driving questions. Students in grades 3-5 were able to choose from 18 different project choices, up from five during the first Day 9, and teachers reported more purposeful engagement during sharing times at the end of the day. Going forward, the Task Force will continue to focus on increasing quality in these areas, including students in designing and developing the next Day 9, and offering professional development and support for using Design Thinking as an approach for projects where 'making' things is a focus.

Day 9 continues to evolve and shift the tides at the American School of Bombay. Teachers and students continue to learn, innovate, and disrupt traditional styles of teaching and learning. The first Day 9 in the Middle School will be on Friday April 4th, 2014. ASB Middle School and Grade 5 teams will partner with NuVu Studio - https://cambridge.nuvustudio.com/discover and their coaches to conduct Day 9 learning projects with a focus on Design Thinking. April 4 is also the elementary school's second Day 9 for this school year.

Day 9 is just one example of how critical elements and trends can come together to form a unique opportunity to create an event of "unusual magnitude". As we continue to learn from the experiences and lessons gained from this innovative day, we hope to see and create more opportunities to shift the tide in education and engage students in powerful learning experiences today.

We look forward to sharing the evolving Day 9 story in the next volume of *Future Forwards*.

Example 5

How Curiosity Found a Home in the Art Studio

(This section is written by Suzie Boss and published in *Future Forwards*, Volume 2)

"Inquiry is the personal path of questioning, investigating, and reasoning that takes us from not knowing to knowing."

— from *Thinking Through Project-Based Learning.*

Good questions are at the heart of the inquiry experience. When investigations are guided by questions that students care about answering, engagement increases. The same goes for teacher learning. Teachers who are willing to ask hard questions about their own practice model what it means to be a continuous, curious learner.

Take the case of Karen Fish, visual art teacher at ASB high school. Earlier this year, the veteran educator found herself wondering about strategies that might deepen student engagement. She was motivated in part by the emphasis on student ownership in the ISTE National Educational Technology Standards for Students. She also was curious how she might make better use of the time at the end of units, when some students finish assignments sooner than others. It's not always the same students who are left "in the gap," as she puts it. "Some are more comfortable with drawing. Others just take off when it's a sculptural project. They work at different speeds on different assignments, and it's unpredictable."

Fish has tried filling the gap by encouraging students to pursue individual interests. "They would start off so excited, but then I could see the motivation going away as soon as we moved on to a new unit [that the teacher assigned]. They had no time to continue working on something they cared about. I wasn't honoring their interests by giving them what they really needed, which was time," she says.

Fish was intrigued, too, by the Curiosity Project, an immersion in student-directed in the elementary school at ASB. The idea was pioneered by Scot Hoffman, now on ASB's R&D team, when he was an elementary teacher. Curiosity Projects involves students exploring topics they are curious about as they participate in an extended homework project. Read more about the Curiosity Project in this Google Doc: (bit.ly/CuriosityProjectsTemplate) and in this Edutopia post (bit.ly/curioushomework).

And so Fish posed this question: What if she modified the Curiosity Project as an in-class assignment for her art students? What might they produce if given the freedom—and time—to explore a visual art style that makes them curious? In the following interview, she reflects on what happened next.

Why did you make this an in-class project, rather than assign as homework?

Karen Fish: If I'm really going to honor students' motivation and interests, I realized I need to give them time. So I handed over 12 class period for this project. That meant shortening some other units and picking up the pace. I thought that would be a good thing. We get too bogged down sometimes. This would be a nice, short unit with a lot of student ownership.

Did students quickly identify what they wanted to work on? How did you help those who struggled to come up with a project idea?

KF: Some did struggle at first. If they seemed a bit lost, I asked them, what do you really care about? One boy wears a baseball cap to school every day. Baseball is clearly his passion. When I pointed that out to him, his eyes got all shiny and he came alive. Another boy, new to the school, said he had only worked in black and white. It turns out he loves the ocean—he's a surfer. So here was a chance for him to use color to explore drawing waves. Other students brought in a specific image or example from an artist who inspires them. The inspiration was different for each student.

How did you structure the project?

KF: I knew I was going to have a lot of kids doing different things. How was I going to give feedback to everybody? We set up a Google Doc and I had them reflect after every class. Then I could respond with resources or individualized instruction. I might share a YouTube video or book with one or show another something about a technique like dry brush.

What was challenging about this for you, as a teacher?

KF: At first, I wasn't sure how much I should get involved. This was supposed to be student-directed learning, right? I wanted to let them find their own way and not keep telling them, here's how you do this. But at first I pulled back too much. I was missing the teachable moments. So I talked with Scot (Hoffman), and he reassured me that it's OK to help them in a project like this. Then I started guiding them more.

What did you notice about students' reflections?

KF: One girl started with a ceramics project. She made candleholders, kind of sculptural but not very challenging. She told me, 'I can make clay fast. I want to try something harder.' So then she tried painting sunflowers, inspired by Monet. There are layers of paint behind the surface of her canvas—a lot of starting, stopping, starting over. She has a lovely sense of textures. She has discovered a clear talent toward painting and she wants to explore this more. She has found a confidence that a lot of kids don't have.

Another girl, new to the school, arrived with very little English. I don't speak Japanese. So we've had to do a lot of gesturing. She showed me a photo of a dock jutting into the ocean, showing a vanishing point. That inspired her. She had to learn techniques to get the sky and clouds just the way she wanted. I was able to provide just-in-time instruction so she could go forward. She's so visually aware—she'll just take my hand and point, show me something she wants to learn to do. And now her English is coming right along, too. She has such a positive attitude toward learning.

How did you assess this project?

KF: Well, I have to grade! I can't give up 12 class periods just for fun. It occurred to me early on that some students had aimed really high. They might not have polished studio projects ready by the end, but they've taken a risk to try something big. I don't want to penalize them for risk taking. Normally, I grade a project 60 percent on the final product and 40 percent on their reflection and investigation—the process. I was honest with the class and told them I had this dilemma about how to grade.

I explained that some students are just flying on the reflection and process part, but the studio work is not coming out how they want yet. Others have fabulous products, but don't like to reflect on their process. I suggested flipping the usual formula, and putting more emphasis on process and reflection. Well, when I said that, some students said, 'Yay!' and others said 'Oh, no.' So I asked them why, and then told them I'd need to go away and think about it.

The solution I came up with is a sliding scale. I've shared the rubric for grading, and it's up to each student to slide the percentages around. How much shall we emphasize your product in grading? How much your process? Each student sets the parameters. That has become something else for them to think about, and I think it's making assessment more valuable. The goal is for everyone to be successful, and to think about what they've set out to accomplish.

What have you noticed about motivation in this project?

KF: Many students have worked harder than they have on any art project before. Some are taking work home and continuing to work on it there. One girl started with an idea of a large digital portrait that she would manipulate with type. She began with one family member, but as she's learning more about technique, she's going on to produce portraits of her entire family. And each one's getting better.

What will you take away from this project into future art assignments?

KF: Everyone's curious about something, aren't they? I've seen such a diversity of projects. I admit, that's been a little scary for me as a teacher. I've had students attempting techniques I know nothing about, especially when it comes to digital tools. But then I get to say, how did you do that? Can you teach me? I think that's a good thing for us all.

What did art students think about the Curiosity Project? Here are a few reflections that they shared while the project was still underway.

John: I'm originally from Santa Barbara, Calif. My whole family surfs. This is my first real art class. I like that I've had the chance to decide what I want to make and how to use my time. I like setting my own goals and reflecting on my own progress. Right now I'm working on a picture of a surfer in the barrel, about to head into a wave. I'm blending pastels to get the  colors just the way I want them, the blues and greens. I know just what they should look like. I've been there myself so many times.

 **Eunji:** I'm painting sunflowers in the style of Monet. He's my favorite artist. I'm happy with how the flowers look but I'm struggling with the pot, getting the color and light right. It's only my second time using acrylics. There are probably three versions on the canvas behind what you see! My mom has a place waiting for this painting on our living room wall.

Meenu: This is a combination of 2D and 3D. I'm drawing on the Japanese style of making everyday objects seem more dramatic. This project has involved a lot of time management. It's all about you and the goals you set for yourself.

When I add the sculpture—the 3D—it will be like a person looking out from a balcony.

Eunji: I'm making a big portrait of my brother's face. He's 10. It's a new style for me. It looks like

scribbling, but I like how it adds texture to the portrait. I kind of panicked when we started this project. I'm not used to coming up with my own ideas. It can be hard to direct myself, to know what to do next.

But I'm enjoying the final product. It think it captures how active my brother is. That's a big part of his personality.

REFERENCES

"A Roadmap for Impact." *Root Capital*. Root Capital. Retrieved. 20 Oct 2013. http://www.rootcapital.org/sites/default/files/downloads/rootcapital_impactroadmap.pdf

"About Us." (2013), *Grameen Bank*. Grameen Bank. Retrieved. 19 Oct 2013. http://www.grameen-info.org/index.php?option=com_content&task=view&id=792&Itemid=759

Amabile, T., & Kramer, S. (2011). *The Progress Principle: Using small wins to ignite joy, engagement, and creativity at work*. Boston, Mass.: Harvard Business Review Press.

Ballinger, C. (1995). Prisoners No More. *Educational Leadership*, 53 (3), 28-31. Retrieved from www.ascd.org

Ballinger, C. and Kneese, C. (2006). *School Calendar Reform, Learning in All Seasons*. Lanham, MD: Rowman & Littlefield Publishers, Inc.

Barthelemy, B. & Dalmagne-Rouge, C. (2013, September 13). *When You're Innovating, Resist Looking for Solutions*. Retrieved June 6, 2014, from (http://blogs.hbr.org/2013/09/when-youre-innovating-resist-l/)

Carson-Dellosa. (2012). *School May Stop for Summer but Learning Never Should*. Greensboro, NC: Carson-Dellosa Publishing, LLC.

Cooper, H. (2003). *Summer Learning Loss: The Problem and Some Solutions*. LD Online. DOI: ED475391

Cunningham, D. (2011*). Improving Teaching with Collaborative Action Research: An ASCD action tool*. Alexandria, Va.: ASCD.

Diaz-Maggioli, G. (2004). *Teacher-Centered Professional Development.* Alexandria, VA: Association for Supervision and Curriculum Development.

Dyer, J., Gregersen, H. B., & Christensen, C. M. (2011). *The Innovator's DNA: Mastering the five skills of disruptive innovators.* Boston, Mass.: Harvard Business Press.

Essential Conditions. (2010). Retrieved May 29, 2015, from http://www.iste.org/standards/essential-conditions

Garmston, R. J., & Zimmerman, D. P. (2013). *Lemons to lemonade: Resolving problems in meetings, workshops, and PLCs.* Corwin Press.

Gergen, C., & Rego, L. (2014, February 19). Educating a New Generation of Entrepreneurial Leaders (SSIR). Retrieved May 12, 2015, from http://www.ssireview.org/blog/entry/educating_a_new_ generation_of_entrepreneurial_leaders

Godin, S. (2010). *Linchpin: Are you indispensable?.* New York: Portfolio.

Harvard Business Review. (2011). *Accelerating Change* [PPT document]. Retrieved April 14, 2015, from https://hbr.org/product/accelerating-change-a-powerpoint-presentation-based-on-the-work-of-john-p-kotter/9467TL-PPT-ENG.index.html

Hattie, J. (1999). Influence on student learning [PDF document]. Retrieved from (https://cdn.auckland.ac.nz/assets/education/hattie/docs/influences-on-student- learning.pdf)

Hattie, J. (2009). *Visible Learning: A synthesis of over 800 meta-analyses relating to achievement.* New York: Routledge.

Heick, Terry. (2014, April 29). "22 Things We Do As Educators That Will Embarrass Us In 25 Years." *TeachThought.* N.p. Retrieved. 1 May 2014.

(http://www.teachthought.com/technology/22-things-educations-will-embarrass-us-25-years/).

Hoffman, S. (2014). Prototyping in Schools. In *Future Forwards: Exploring frontiers in education at the American School of Bombay, Volume* 2 (pp. 11-16). Mumbai: American School of Bombay.

Hoffman, S. (2014). The Workbook: An action research tool for an always beta school. In *Future Forwards: Exploring frontiers in education at the American School of Bombay*. Mumbai, India: American School of Bombay.

Institute For The Future. (2008). *The Future of Making*. Retrieved April 14, 2015, from http://www.iftf. org/uploads/media/SR-1154%20TH%202008%20Maker%20Map.pdf

Kipling, Rudyard. "If.". *Poems & Poets*. Poetry Foundation. Retrieved 15 April 2014.

Kotter, John P. (2014). *Accelerate: Building strategic agility for a faster-moving world*. Boston, MA: Harvard Business Review.

Lopez, S. J. (2013). *Making Hope Happen: Create the future you want for yourself and others*. New York: Atria Books.

Marx, G. (2014). *21 Trends for the 21st Century: Out of the trenches and into the future.* Bethesda MD: Education Week Press.

McNicholas, Kym. (2011) "16-Year Old Social Entrepreneur Wins National Competition Vowing To Reduce World Waste." *Forbes*. Retrieved. 11 Dec. 2013. http://www.forbes.com/sites/kymmcnicholas/2011/10/07/16-year-old-social-entrepreneur-wins-national-competition-vowing-to-reduce-world-waste/

National Center for Summer Learning. (2009). Summer Learning Bulletin, April 2009. Baltimore, MD: Johns Hopkins University School of Education

National Summer Learning Association. (2009). More Than a Hunch: Kids Lose Learning Skills Over the Summer Months - interview with Professor H. Cooper. NSLA Research in Brief. Baltimore, MD: www.summerlearning.org

Perpetual Beta. (2013, June 29). In Wikipedia, the Free Encyclopedia. Retrieved 09:48, December 9, 2013, from (http://en.wikipedia.org/w/index.php?title=Perpetual_beta&oldid=562081742)

Peters, T. J. (1987). *Thriving on Chaos: Handbook for a management revolution*. New York: Knopf.

Reading is Fundamental. (2009). Primer on Summer Learning Loss. Washington, DC: www.rif.org

Rogers, E. M. (2003). *The Diffusion of Innovations*. New York: Simon & Schuster.

Schrage, M. (2014).*The Innovator's Hypothesis: How cheap experiments are worth more than good ideas*. Boston: MIT Press.

Shields, C. and Oberg, S. (2009). Balanced Calendar Schools: Combining Structural Change and Transformative Leadership. In C. Kneese and C. Ballinger (Eds.), *Balancing the School Calendar* (pp. 40). Lanham, MD: Rowman & Littlefield Publishers, Inc.

Siemens, G. (2006). *Knowing Knowledge*. Lulu.com.

Social Entrepreneurship in India. (2014, August 1). Retrieved May 12, 2015, from http://www.oifc.in/ social-entrepreneurship-india

T Brown. (2009, July 30). *Change by Design*. Retrieved from https://www.youtube.com/ watch?v=LMzUnYfACeU

Van Velsor, E., & Wright, J. (2012). *Expanding the Leadership Equation: Developing Next-Generation Leaders*. A White Paper. *Center for Creative Leadership (NJ1).*

Venkataswamy, G. "The Beginning." *Aravind Eye Care*. Aravind Eye Care System, Retrieved. 20 Oct 2013. http://www.aravind.org/aboutus/genesis.aspx

Wagner, T. & Compton, R. A. (2012). *Creating Innovators: The making of young people who will change the world.* New York: Scribner.